D1356118

TRADITIONAL

JAMS &
PRESERVES

TRADITIONAL

JAMS &
PRESERVES

Eve Parker

AURA

This edition published in 2012
by Baker & Taylor (UK) Limited,
Bicester, Oxfordshire

Copyright © 2012 Arcturus Publishing Limited
26/27 Bickels Yard, 151–153 Bermondsey Street
London SE1 3HA

ISBN: 978-1-90723-127-8
AD002225EN

Printed in China

CONTENTS

INTRODUCTION

There's nothing that sets the taste buds tingling more than the sight and scent of freshly made jam or preserve. While it's quick and easy to grab a jar of something sweet or spicy from the supermarket shelves, once you have made and tasted your own preserves you'll realize that there is absolutely no comparison.

A BRIEF HISTORY OF PRESERVING

Today, eating jams and other preserves is just an enjoyable part of daily life, but to our ancestors it was a necessity – a way of making food last in the absence of the modern conveniences to which we are accustomed. Nothing went to waste, and people needed to find ways of keeping fruit and vegetables fresh to provide a food supply through the winter months.

Although the precise origin of jam remains uncertain, we do know that it has a very long history. There is reference to jams in the first-ever book of recipes, entitled *Of Culinary Matters*, written by the Roman gastronome Marcus Gavius Apicius in the 1st century AD. He had discovered that by adding a sweetener such as honey to fruit and boiling it at a high temperature, the fruit could be preserved for eating all year round. Before that time, fruits and vegetables would be laid out in the heat of the sun, or hung up to dry. In countries without reliably long hours of sunshine, smoking was employed to speed up the drying process.

The use of sugar as a preservative wasn't discovered until the 12th century, when cane sugar was introduced to Europe by Crusaders returning from the Middle East. Although it remained too much of a luxury for the majority of people, there was

a great demand for sugar among the wealthy and the trade in it increased as delicious uses for this new ingredient were discovered, not least the preservation of fruit. The magnificent banquets laid on by Louis XIV of France always finished with an assortment of fruit preserves presented on silver platters. All the preserves on the King's table would have been made with fruit from the royal gardens and glasshouses.

By Tudor times there was a wide range of jam recipes available to cooks, one in particular was for quince and medlar, the latter a fruit that seems to have lost favour in modern times. But it wasn't until the 19th century that preserving became really popular and was considered to be a culinary art. Larders and pantries were filled with jar after jar of jams, jellies, pickles, chutneys and marmalades to be enjoyed during the lean winter months. As fruit and vegetables contain many vitamins, preserves were seen as a way to supplement the diet in times of food shortage.

It is believed that marmalade came into existence during the 16th century. Although the story is a little far-fetched, the discovery of marmalade is attributed to the physician of Mary, Queen of Scots. It is said that when the Queen complained of *mal de mer* (seasickness), her doctor tried a combination of orange and sugar to settle her stomach. Whether it worked or not isn't known, but she liked the flavour so much that she asked her cooks to produce more of this delicious concoction. The name it was given derived from the Portuguese word for quince, *marmelo*.

Marmalade would have been an excellent way of providing sailors with vitamin C when fresh fruit wasn't available and it is believed it was given to men on board merchant vessels to help prevent scurvy and other illnesses. Today, of course, we view marmalade primarily as a spread to put on toast at breakfast.

As kitchen appliances improved and the majority of households gained the luxury of fridges and freezers, the practice of making preserves started to dwindle. Housewives no longer needed to find ways of preserving fruit and vegetables, and if a preserve was wanted it was much easier to go to the local supermarket and buy a jar.

Luckily, the art of preserving is coming back into fashion as people are encouraged to turn to some of the more traditional ways of cooking. By making your own preserves, you are in control of the amount of sugar in them and can ensure that they do not contain any artificial colourings or flavours. Once you experience the satisfaction of producing your own jams and chutneys, you will never look back.

This book explains the process of making preserves and is full of interesting and delicious recipes for you to try. It describes the equipment and ingredients you will need and shows how to make sure your jars of goodies keep for the longest possible time. Read all the instructions carefully before you begin, then dive in and enjoy yourself – you will soon wonder how you managed to survive without a cupboard full of homemade jams, jellies, chutneys, pickles and marmalades!

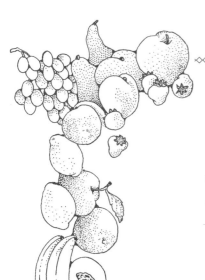

PART 1

GETTING STARTED

The beauty of making preserves is that you won't need to go out and buy a lot of expensive equipment. You will probably find you have the majority of the utensils you require already in your kitchen cupboard, and those you may need to shop for are relatively inexpensive.

EQUIPMENT

This section explains the items of equipment that will ensure the job of making preserves becomes that much easier, helping you to find success every time.

PRESERVING PAN

The preserving or jam pan is probably the most important piece of equipment you will need. For small quantities, a stainless steel saucepan is fine as long as it has a thick base to prevent the jam from sticking and burning. For larger quantities, invest in a good-quality preserving pan which will last you a lifetime.

A preserving pan is specially designed with a wide top to allow for rapid evaporation of liquid.

This means that setting point (see page 23) can be reached more quickly. The pan should be large enough to allow the contents to boil rapidly without bubbling over, so a minimum capacity of 9 litres/16 pints is advisable. It is also essential that the pan has a thick base. Avoid using copper pans, as they are unsuitable for preserves that contain any acidity, such as recipes with lemon juice or vinegar; both the flavour and colour of the jam will be spoilt. Enamel pans are not suitable either, as they burn easily and do not conduct heat efficiently enough.

Preserving pans come with either a large handle over the top or a handle on each side. Both of these are suitable, so it's a matter of personal choice.

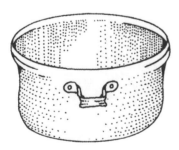

JARS

You can use any type of glass or preserving jar as long as it's not damaged. The main priority is that it is sterilized (see page 15), dry and hot before potting up, as wet jars may cause the preserve to go mouldy prematurely and cold ones could crack when the hot preserve is poured into them.

If you are making the preserve for yourself, use smaller jars so that the jam or pickle will stay fresh even if it takes you a couple of weeks to eat it. Don't throw away the glass jars after you have eaten the contents – just wash, rinse and sterilize them.

Getting into the habit of keeping all your glass jars will ensure you always have a plentiful supply of containers. Avoid using jars with very narrow necks as you will find it difficult to transfer the hot jam into the jar even if you are using a funnel. Glass Kilner jars with rubber seals, although more expensive, are ideal for making preserves as they are wide-necked, totally

non-corrosive and can be used time and time again.

LIDS AND COVERS

If your jars come with twist-top lids these are fine, but you can use paper or cellophane covers tied on with string or elastic bands if necessary. However, paper and cling film are not vinegar-proof, so cannot be used for any recipe containing vinegar. Kilner jars come with their own glass lids that are permanently attached with a rubber seal.

WAX CIRCLES

To help prevent mould from forming on the surface of the jam, you can buy specially cut waxed circles in assorted sizes that you drop on top of the jam before finally sealing the jars.

SPOONS

You will need a long-handled wooden spoon for stirring and a slotted metal spoon for removing scum from the surface while the jam is cooking. It's important that all spoons used for jam making have long handles to prevent you burning your hands. Keep separate wooden spoons for sweet and savoury preserves and avoid metal spoons when stirring, as these conduct heat and may alter the colour of the finished preserve.

LABELS
These are particularly important if you intend to make a wide variety of preserves because they will tell you exactly what each jar contains and when the preserve was made. You can buy labels from a kitchen shop or alternatively make your own like the one below. Labels add a lovely finishing touch to jars of

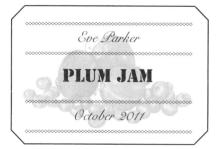

Eve Parker

PLUM JAM

October 2011

preserves when you give them away as presents, so be creative with your design.

SUGAR THERMOMETER
This is not essential, as you can test for setting point using other methods (see page 23), but a thermometer will definitely make your life easier and help you obtain the perfect setting point. Choose one specifically designed for the job, with a clip or handle that can be hooked over the side of the preserving pan. You also need to make sure it goes up to at least 110°C/230°F.

MUSLIN
Certain recipes require a herb or spice bag. This can be made by tying several layers of muslin together with a piece of string. When you are making marmalade these little bags are also useful to hold the pips and peel to add more pectin to a recipe.

If you don't want to go to the expense of buying a jelly bag (see below), a piece of muslin makes a perfectly good substitute (see page 17).

JELLY BAG

When you are making jellies, it's essential to strain the fruit pulp carefully so the final jelly is clear and free of any pulp debris. If you feel you would like to make jelly on a regular basis it's worth acquiring a specially made jelly bag which will either have four hanging loops or come with its own convenient frame. A jelly bag is usually made from nylon and can be washed and used repeatedly.

FUNNELS

It's definitely worth buying a funnel, as this makes the job of potting your preserves much easier. Choose one with a wide tube to allow any larger chunks to pass through, but not so wide that it won't fit into the top of your smallest jar. You need one made either of stainless steel or heatproof plastic.

BOWLS

A variety of non-corrosive bowls in different sizes come in handy when a recipe calls for soaking, marinading or mixing.

CHOPPING BOARDS

It's advisable to have at least two chopping boards so that you can use one for fruit and the other for stronger ingredients such as chillies, onions and garlic. This will ensure that one flavour won't contaminate another. Wooden chopping boards also come in handy as a surface for potting as they won't cool the jars down too quickly.

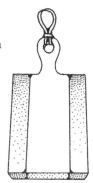

SIEVES AND COLANDERS

Use only plastic sieves and colanders when draining acidic preserves or fruit. If you use metal ones they can give your jam or pickle a slightly metallic tang.

LADLE AND JUG

Ladles are ideal for transferring hot liquid when potting your preserve. You will need one made from stainless steel or heatproof plastic and preferably with a lip, as this makes pouring easier. A glass jug can also be used to transfer the hot liquid.

GRATER

A box grater is probably the best type to use as it has a number of different surfaces – recipes may call for either fine or coarse grating. Many box graters come with a slicing blade as well, which can be useful.

KNIVES, VEGETABLE PEELER AND STONER

Ordinary sharp kitchen knives will be adequate for preparing

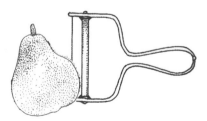

fruit and vegetables, while a vegetable peeler can come in handy for removing zest. The ones with a swivel action allow you to follow the contour of the fruit so that the peel can be removed thinly. Stoners are useful when you have a large quantity of fiddly stones to remove from fruit such as cherries. It is almost impossible to keep the fruit whole when trying to remove the stone with a knife.

SCALES AND SPOONS

A pair of accurate scales is an important piece of the jam maker's equipment. Digital scales that show both metric and imperial are probably the best kind to use as you can set them back to zero after you have placed a container on them.

Some preserving recipes may call for very small amounts, such as a teaspoon or half a teaspoon. If you don't have a set of measuring spoons, a level teaspoon of average size is a fairly accurate measure.

STERILIZING

If you have gone to the trouble of making a preserve, you don't want it to go mouldy a few days later. To make sure of the success and longevity of the finished product, you need to clean and sterilize all jars thoroughly.

Before you start any new recipe, make sure you have a large enough number of jars so that you don't have to stop in the middle of potting up in order to search for more containers.

Even if all your jars appear to be really clean, it's important to sterilize them to destroy any harmful bacteria. First check them over for signs of cracks or other damage, then wash them thoroughly in hot, soapy water.

Rinse them under clean, running water to remove the soap, then stand them upside down to drain.

There are several different ways to sterilize glass jars and bottles and each works equally well, so the choice is up to you. Consider each of the methods given overleaf carefully, as some of them may not be appropriate, especially if you don't have a dishwasher or microwave.

METHOD 1: IN THE OVEN

After you have washed the jars, stand them on a baking tray lined with kitchen paper. Make sure none of the jars are touching and rest any lids loosely on top – do not tighten them. Put the jars in a cold oven and then heat it to 110°C/230°F/gas mark ¼ and leave them in the oven with the door closed for 30 minutes. Fill the jars while they are still hot – if you are not ready to do this, cover them with a clean tea towel and heat again before use.

METHOD 2: IN BOILING WATER

Find a heatproof container that's wide and deep enough to hold the jars in a single layer. Pour enough hot water into the pan to cover the jars completely, place the pan on the top of your cooker and bring the water to the boil. Keep the water at a rolling boil for 10 minutes, then turn off the heat and leave the jars in the water until it stops bubbling. Protecting your hands carefully, remove the jars and turn them upside down on a clean tea towel to drain. Fill the jars while they are still hot. Remember to include any lids in the boiling process so that they are sterilized too.

METHOD 3: IN THE DISHWASHER

If you own a dishwasher, this is by far the easiest method and you can sterilize a large number of jars at a time. Simply put the containers and lids into the dishwasher and set the machine to the hottest setting. This will include drying at the end of the programme.

- - - - - - - - - - - - - - - -

JELLY BAG

If you are making jellies and you need to use a jelly bag, it must also be sterilized by boiling for 10 minutes before use.

- - - - - - - - - - - - - - - -

METHOD 4: IN THE MICROWAVE

Sterilizing jars in a microwave is quick and ideal if you only want to do a few jars at a time. Don't use very large jars – small, squat ones are best. Half-fill the clean jars with water, place them on the turntable and run your microwave to its highest setting for a minute. Remove the jars, using an oven glove to protect your hand, tip out the water and turn them upside down on a clean tea towel to drain.

METHOD 5: STERILIZING SOLUTION

If you are making a strongly flavoured chutney or pickle you can use sterilizing tablets. Dilute the tablets according to the manufacturer's instructions and immerse the jars for the amount of time given. Drain and dry thoroughly before using. As sterilizing solution can leave a slight aftertaste, this method is not recommended for some of the more delicately flavoured jams and preserves.

- - - - - - - - - - - - - - - - - -

IMPROVISE

A piece of sterilized muslin will stand in for a jelly bag if you don't have one. Use it doubled to line a sieve or strainer, or simply tie it to the legs of an upturned kitchen stool (see below) with a bowl placed beneath it.

- - - - - - - - - - - - - - - - - -

BASIC STEPS IN MAKING JAM

Making jam is not difficult, but there are a few basic rules to follow if you want to achieve the best clarity, colour and consistency.

The most important thing when you are making jams, and indeed conserves and jellies too, is your choice of fruit. Don't assume this is a good way to use up bruised windfalls or fruit that is badly damaged, as the success or failure of jam depends entirely on the quality of the fruit.

STEP 1: PREPARING THE FRUIT

Choose your fruit carefully – only fresh, firm and just ripe is acceptable. Never use fruit that is over-ripe as this will have lost most of its pectin, which means that your jam will not reach setting point. (For more information on pectin, see pages 20–21.)

Wash the fruit and check it over carefully for any signs of bruising or decay. Remove the stems and cores from soft fruits such as strawberries. Smaller berries such as currants or elderberries should be removed from their stalks. This can be done quite quickly by simply taking a fork and slipping the stalks between the prongs.

Harder fruits such as apples and pears will need to be peeled, cored and cut into pieces. Cherries can either be cut in half and the stones removed with a sharp knife, or left whole and the stones removed with a proprietary stoner. Apricots, peaches, plums and nectarines should be cut in half and the stone removed with a sharp knife.

If you are using rose hips, you will need to remove the seeds first. Simply halve the hips and push the seeds out using the handle of a teaspoon.

TOP TIP

If you want to make a larger quantity than the recipe suggests, don't just double the amount of the ingredients as your jam won't cook to the setting stage in the time given in the recipe. Instead, make the recipe twice in two separate preserving pans. Likewise, don't attempt to cut the recipe in half or you will encounter a similar problem with the setting time.

STEP 2: SOFTENING THE FRUIT

After you have prepared the fruit and weighed it carefully, the next stage is to pre-cook the flesh to help break it down, to lose some of the moisture and soften the skins. Depending on the fruit being used, you may need to add a little water at this stage. Juicy fruits such as strawberries, raspberries and rhubarb contain enough liquid of their own, but other harder fruits require varying amounts.

Put the fruit into your preserving pan and bring it to the boil. Reduce the heat and simmer gently until the fruit has turned to a pulp and reduced in quantity to approximately one-third. Avoid the temptation to stir the fruit during this stage.

STEP 3: ADDING ACID

Acid is a vital requirement when making jam and this is released from fruits during the first stage of cooking. Some fruits contain a high quantity of acid, while others are low in it; in the case of the latter, lemon juice is added to compensate for the lack of acid naturally present. Allow 2 tablespoons of lemon juice for every 900g/2lb of fruit that is low in acid.

Fruits high in acid:
- cooking or sour apples
- grapefruit
- lemons
- limes
- oranges
- pineapples
- quince
- sour grapes
- sour peaches
- sour plums
- tangerines
- tomatoes

Fruits low in acid:
- apricots
- blackberries
- blueberries
- cherries
- eating or sweet apples
- elderberries
- figs
- gooseberries
- mangoes
- nectarines
- raspberries
- strawberries
- sweet peaches
- sweet plums

STEP 4: ADDING PECTIN

After the fruit has been reduced to a pulp, but before the sugar is added, it is necessary to determine the amount of pectin present (see the box opposite). Pectin is a natural, soluble polysaccharide fibre found in fruit and acts as a setting agent for the finished jam. Cooking fruit brings out the gelling ability of pectin, but overcooking can destroy it. All fruits contain a certain amount of pectin but some have more than others, for example:

High in pectin:
- blackcurrants
- clementines
- cooking apples
- crab apples
- cranberries

- damsons
- gooseberries
- grapes
- lemons
- limes
- oranges
- plums
- quince
- redcurrants
- tangerines
- unripe blackberries

Medium in pectin:
- apricots
- greengages
- loganberries
- raspberries

Low in pectin:
- blueberries
- cherries
- elderberries
- peaches
- rhubarb
- ripe blackberries
- strawberries

It is essential for making jam that the pectin is combined with the right amount of sugar. The sugar absorbs water from the fruit which, when combined with citric acid, stimulates the activity of pectin.

If you are using fruits that are particularly low in pectin, you can

---

TESTING FOR PECTIN

Take 1 teaspoon of fruit juice and put it inside a glass jar to cool. Add 3 teaspoons of methylated spirit, place the lid on the jar and shake it well. After a minute, pour the liquid into a glass.

- If the liquid has formed one large clot it means the juice is high in pectin;
- If the liquid has formed a few smaller clots it means there is less pectin but the juice is still adequate;
- If the liquid has many small clots you will need to add pectin.

---

make up the deficiency by doing one of the following:

1. Mixing a low-pectin fruit with a high-pectin one, for example cooking apples with blackberries.

2. Using pectin in a liquid or powdered form which you can purchase from most major supermarkets.

3. Adding lemon juice or citric acid to your recipe.

4. Adding pectin stock – see the recipe below.

Pectin stock

900g/2lb cooking apples
420ml/15fl oz water

1. Roughly chop the apples, including the peel, cores and pips. Place them in a heavy-based saucepan and cover with cold water. Bring to the boil, then reduce the heat and put the lid on the saucepan. Allow the mixture to simmer for about 40 minutes or until the apples have become soft and pulpy.

2. Pour the mixture into a sterilized jelly bag or a double thickness of muslin inside a sieve and leave to drain into a jug or bowl for at least 2 hours.

3. Transfer the strained apple juice into a clean saucepan and boil for about 20 minutes or until the liquid has reduced by one-third.

4. Transfer the pectin stock into sterilized jars and store in the refrigerator. It will keep for a week in the fridge, or up to 4 months if you freeze it. To use frozen pectin stock, allow it to defrost at room temperature or overnight in the refrigerator.

As a guideline, use 120–250ml/ 4–8fl oz of pectin stock to every 900g/2lb of fruit. If you are using powdered pectin, the suggested amount is 15g/½oz to every 900g/2lb of fruit.

STEP 5: ADDING SUGAR

Most types of sugar can be used for making jams and conserves, but two are especially designed for the purpose. Preserving sugar is ideal for fruits that are naturally high in pectin; the sugar crystals are larger than those in granulated sugar, which means they dissolve rapidly. It also produces less froth, resulting in a clearer preserve.

In the case of a jam made from fruits that are low in pectin, a jam sugar will often be specified in the recipe; jam sugar contains natural pectin, which ensures that your jam will set.

In some recipes, caster or granulated sugar may be given when no extra pectin is required. The recipes in this book have been carefully tested, so always follow the amount and type of sugar recommended.

To get the best results, warm the sugar gently in the oven before adding it to the preserving pan so that it doesn't lower the temperature of the contents. Once the sugar has been added, you will need to stir constantly over a medium heat until the sugar has dissolved completely and to avoid the mixture burning or sticking to the base of the pan.

When you are happy that the sugar has dissolved, increase the heat and bring the mixture back to the boil. You can then reduce the heat very slightly, but you will need to retain an active boil to reach setting point. At this stage, stir the jam just enough to stop it sticking, otherwise you risk mixing too much of the scum into the jam.

The time taken to reach setting point will vary according to the type of fruit used. If the boiling time is too short, the jam won't set; if it is too long, the jam will become dark and sticky and lose much of its fresh flavour. Stop boiling as soon as setting point has been reached.

STEP 6: TEST FOR SETTING POINT

There are three ways of testing for setting point – the flake test, the wrinkle test and with a sugar thermometer. As some jams can set very quickly, check early in the cooking time. When testing for set, take the pan off the heat and do one of the following:

Flake test

Stir the jam and put a small amount on a wooden spoon. Leave it for a couple of minutes to cool, then turn the spoon on its side. If the jam has reached setting point it should run off the side of the spoon slowly in one flat flake. If it is not ready it will run off the spoon too quickly and you will need to continue boiling the jam.

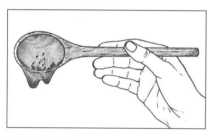

Wrinkle test

Place a saucer or small plate in the refrigerator to chill. Take the preserving pan off the heat, drop a little jam onto the saucer and leave to cool for about a minute. Gently push the jam with your finger; if the surface wrinkles, the jam has reached setting point. If it wrinkles only slightly, return the pan to the heat and

cook for a further 2–3 minutes, then test again.

Using a sugar thermometer

Put the sugar thermometer in hot water, then place it in the preserve. To get an accurate reading, stir the jam gently with the thermometer for a couple of minutes, making sure you don't touch the base of the pan. Jams and marmalades reach setting point when the temperature reads 105°C/220°F.

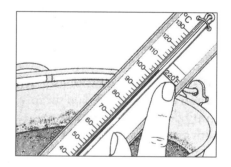

STEP 7: REMOVING THE SCUM

Once you are happy that the jam has reached setting point, take it off the heat and leave it to stand, without stirring, for about 10 minutes. If there is any scum lying on the surface, remove it carefully with a slotted spoon and then drop a knob of butter (about the size of a walnut) into the mixture to disperse any scum that remains.

STEP 8: POTTING UP

Now you are ready to pot up your jam in dry, hot, sterilized jars. Stand the jars on a tray or surface that is easy to wipe clean, as it is bound to get sticky. Using a ladle or jug and a wide-necked funnel is the easiest way to minimize spills. Make sure you fill the jars right to the top to allow for shrinkage. Use a damp cloth to wipe off any excess jam on the outside of the jars and immediately place a waxed disc on the surface of the jam, waxed side down, taking care that it doesn't wrinkle.

Seal with a lid while the jam is still hot to ensure that you have an airtight seal. If you don't have a lid for your jars, cover them with paper or cling film circles fixed with an elastic band or a piece of string.

If you're giving your jam as a present, it's a nice idea to decorate the top with a circle of fabric over the lid, tied with a piece of ribbon. Alternatively, if it's a Christmas gift, use some wrapping paper and tuck a holly leaf inside the ribbon to make it look festive.

STEP 9: LABELLING AND STORING

Leave the jam to cool before putting on the label, otherwise you might find it peels off. Don't forget to write the date on which you made the jam – this will remind you which jars should be used first. Store the jars in dry, dark and cool conditions to maximize the shelf life of the jam; if it's left in the light or in a damp atmosphere, mould can develop on the surface. Stored properly, it can keep for up to 6 months.

TROUBLESHOOTING

However much care you have taken at each stage of making your jam, you may experience problems at first and feel that the end product is disappointing. By identifying the cause, you should be able to make a perfect batch next time.

PROBLEM	SOLUTION
Poor setting	— If you find the jam isn't setting when the estimated time is reached, remove the pan from the heat and add 2 teaspoons of citric acid, or the juice of a small lemon. — If the jam hasn't set after it has cooled in the jar, tip it back into a clean preserving pan and boil again, adding the juice of a small lemon. — Check to see that the jam has the correct ratio of sugar to its acid and pectin content.
Mould forming on surface	— This could indicate insufficient cooking at the preliminary stage, or an incorrect amount of sugar in proportion to the fruit. — The jam has not been stored in cool, dry, dark conditions.

PROBLEM	SOLUTION
Mould forming on surface	— The jam was potted while it was warm rather than hot. Open the pot and remove the mould and a thick layer of the jam with a clean teaspoon. Keep the jam in the refrigerator and eat as soon as possible.
Bubbles on the surface	— Bubbles on the top of the jam mean it is starting to ferment. This indicates that there is too little sugar, or that the jam has been stored in a warm place, or the pots were not sealed tightly enough.
Crystallization	— This is usually caused by using too much sugar, or not dissolving it properly before bringing the jam to the boil. It can also happen if you add the acid after the sugar rather than before. There is no remedy to crystallization, but the jam will still be edible, if a little crunchy!
Shrinkage	— If you find the jam has started to shrink away from the sides of the jar, one possible cause is that it has been over-boiled; it can also be the result of not creating an airtight seal when potting up. Putting a fresh cover on the jars will put a stop to any further evaporation and shrinkage.

PROBLEM	SOLUTION
Fruit floating to the top	— If you find the fruit has floated to the top after you have taken the jam off the heat, allow it to cool for 15 minutes and then give it a good stir before putting it into pots.
Jam dull or too dark	— This is caused by overcooking at the preliminary stage either before or after adding the sugar. It can also mean that the jam has been boiled for too long after it has reached setting point.
Jam has faded	— This usually means that the jam has been stored for too long or the storage place was too warm. Red fruits such as strawberries and raspberries are especially vulnerable to fading.

PART 2

JAMS & CONSERVES

There's no better way to preserve the fresh flavour of summer and autumn fruits than by turning them into jams and conserves to be enjoyed all year round. These aren't just for breakfast toast or scones at tea time – they can also used as fillings for sponge cakes, toppings for pancakes and as sauces for steamed puddings.

JAM OR CONSERVE?

There isn't a great deal of difference between jams and conserves, though the latter tend to be found mainly at farmer's markets and among the more expensive jams on supermarket shelves.

Conserves have a softer set than jam and contain whole or larger pieces of fruit. The fruit remains firmer because it is left to soak in a sugar solution to draw out the natural liquid. This means it requires a shorter cooking time. You need to choose fruit that is only just ripe; the pieces need to be roughly the same size so that they cook at the same rate.

Not all fruits are suitable for making conserves. Those with tough outer skins will not soften even after lengthy soaking in sugar syrup. Strawberries, raspberries, apricots, melons and rhubarb all make excellent conserves, but if you want to make this luxurious type of jam you will need to allow plenty of time for the preparation stage. Conserves cannot be rushed!

If you would like to make a really special conserve, you can complement the flavour of the fruit by adding a liqueur such as apricot brandy to an apricot conserve, or ginger wine to a melon one. Choose the flavours you feel will go best with the fruit and you may come up with a new, winning combination.

Although it isn't spelled out each time in the recipes, don't forget to test the pectin level of your fruit (see page 21). If you're in doubt regarding any of the steps in the recipes, refer back to the Getting Started section on pages 10–28, which should answer most of the queries you may have. You'll find that with a little practice at making preserves, all the various stages will become second nature to you.

APPLE & ELDERFLOWER JAM

In the early summer months, when the sweet smell of elderflower permeates the air, try picking a few heads of the old country plant to complement the flavour of apples in this delicious jam.

INGREDIENTS *Makes 1.35–1.8kg/ 3–4lb*

1kg/2¼lb cooking apples, peeled, cored and diced
500ml/16fl oz elderflower heads
400ml/14fl oz water
500g/1lb 2oz preserving sugar, warmed

METHOD

1. Rinse the elderflowers to remove any dirt or insects, then shake dry. Pull the flowers from the stalks and tie them inside a square of muslin to make a bag. Attach a piece of string to the bag so that you can tie it to the edge of the preserving pan.

2. After preparation, you should have approximately 750g/1lb 10oz of apple. Place in the preserving pan together with the bag containing the elderflowers.

3. Add the water and bring the contents of the pan to a simmer. Cook gently for 20 minutes or until the apple has formed a soft pulp.

4. Add the sugar and stir until it has completely dissolved. Bring to the boil and cook for 20 minutes, making sure that the jam is bubbling on the surface. Stir every 5 minutes to prevent it from sticking to the bottom of the pan. As soon as it starts to thicken, start to test for set.

5. Once you are happy that the jam has reached setting point, pour it into four 450g/1lb hot, sterilized jars, add a waxed disc to each one and screw the lids on tightly. Wipe the outside of the jars with a warm, damp cloth and leave to cool before labelling and storing.

APPLE, RHUBARB & GINGER JAM

The flavours in this jam complement one another beautifully.
It is also a perfect way to use up a glut of rhubarb from the garden.

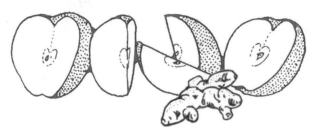

INGREDIENTS *Makes 2.2kg/5lb*
5cm/2in fresh root ginger
800g/1¾lb rhubarb, cut into
   small slices
200g/7oz cooking apples, peeled,
   cored and diced
90ml/3fl oz water
1kg/2¼lb jam sugar, warmed

METHOD
1. Remove the skin from the
ginger and grate the flesh on
the coarse side of the grater.
2. Put the rhubarb, apple and
ginger into a preserving pan
with the water and cook over
a medium heat until the mixture
is soft and pulpy.

3. Add the sugar and stir
constantly until it has completely
dissolved. Turn up the heat and
bring the mixture to a gentle
boil. Cook for about 10 minutes,
then start to test for setting point.
4. Once you are happy that
the jam is ready for potting up,
pour it into sterilized jars, cover
the surface with a waxed disc
and immediately seal with a
lid. Leave the jam to cool before
adding labels.

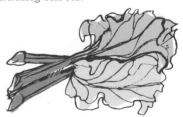

APRICOT JAM

This delicious and popular jam makes a wonderful breakfast treat spread liberally on warm croissants.

INGREDIENTS *Makes 1.3kg/3lb*
1.5kg/3lb 3oz ripe apricots
200ml/7fl oz apple juice
1kg/2¼lb preserving sugar,
   warmed
the juice of 1 lemon
knob of butter (about 15g/½oz)
1 tbsp apricot brandy (optional)

METHOD

1. Halve the apricots and remove the stones. Chop the flesh into small pieces and place in the preserving pan with the apple juice. Bring to the boil, then reduce the heat to a simmer and cook for 10 minutes or until the apricots are soft.

2. Stir in the sugar and lemon juice and cook over a moderate heat, stirring continuously until the sugar has completely dissolved.

3. Increase the heat, simmer gently for 20 minutes, then remove from the heat and test for setting point.

4. Once you are happy the jam is ready, stir in the butter until it melts. Add the apricot brandy (if using), stir and then pour into hot, sterilized jars. Seal, label and store for 2 weeks before eating.

TOP TIP

If you want to give this jam an even richer flavour, crack a few of the apricot kernels and remove the nut in the middle. Put a nut in each jar before pouring in the jam to give the preserve a subtle, almost almond flavour.

BLACKBERRY & APPLE JAM

Hedgerow fruit should never go to waste. Making blackberries into jam is a perfect way to make the most of their full flavour.

INGREDIENTS *Makes 1.5kg/3lb 3oz*
500g/1lb 2oz ripe blackberries
500g/1lb 2oz cooking apples,
    peeled, cored and diced
the juice of 1 lemon
100ml/3½fl oz water
1kg/2¼lb preserving sugar,
    warmed

METHOD
1. Soak the blackberries in cold water for 15 minutes to remove any dirt or insects. Hull the berries and place them in a preserving pan with the apples, lemon juice and water. Cook over a medium heat, simmering gently for 10–15 minutes or until the fruit is soft.
2. Add the sugar to the pan and stir until it has completely dissolved.
3. Turn up the heat and boil the jam rapidly for 5 minutes.

Remove the pan from the heat and check to see whether the jam has reached setting point. If not, return to the heat for 2–3 minutes and check again, repeating until it is ready.
4. Once you are happy the jam has reached setting point, remove from the heat and pot up into hot, sterilized jars. Seal the jars immediately and label when the contents are cool.

BLACKCURRANT JAM

This jam has a rich, dark colour and a strong, almost tart flavour which goes exceptionally well with scones and cream.

INGREDIENTS *Makes 1.35kg/3lb*
1.35kg/3lb blackcurrants
grated zest and juice of 1 orange
500ml/16fl oz water
1.35kg/3lb granulated sugar,
    warmed
knob of butter (about 15g/½oz)

METHOD

1. Remove any stalks from the blackcurrants, then rinse them in cold water.

2. Put the blackcurrants into a preserving pan with the zest and juice of the orange and the water. Cook over a medium heat until the fruit is really soft. This stage is important as the fruit will not soften once the sugar has been added.

3. Add the warmed sugar and cook on a low heat for about 15 minutes, stirring continuously until it has dissolved completely.

Check to see whether the sugar has dissolved by running your finger over the back of the spoon – if it feels grainy, cook for a little longer.

4. Once the sugar has dissolved, turn up the heat and boil the jam rapidly for 10 minutes. Remove it from the heat and test for setting point. If it is not ready, continue to boil for a further 5 minutes and test again.

5. Once the jam has reached setting point, add the butter and stir to disperse any scum that may have formed on the surface.

6. Pour the jam into hot, sterilized jars, add a waxed disc to the top and then seal immediately. Wipe the outside of the jars with a warm, damp cloth and leave the jam to cool before adding labels.

CHERRY CONSERVE

Cherry conserve is delicious on tea-time scones and other sweet treats, but try it too as an accompaniment for roast duck.

INGREDIENTS *Makes 1kg/2¹/4lb*
1kg/2¼lb black cherries
the zest and juice of 2 lemons
1 cinnamon stick, broken in half
150ml/5fl oz water
500g/1lb 2oz jam sugar, warmed
1 tbsp kirsch liqueur (optional)

METHOD

1. Remove the stones from the cherries using a preparatory stoner. Chop half the quantity of cherries into quarters but leave the remainder whole. Place the prepared fruit in a preserving pan. Add the lemon zest and juice, cinnamon stick and water.
2. Bring the mixture to a gentle boil and then reduce the heat so that the fruit simmers for 20 minutes, or until the whole cherries have softened.
3. Add the sugar and stir continuously until it has completely dissolved. Increase the heat and boil rapidly for 4–5 minutes or until the conserve is softly set. For a special treat, stir in the kirsch liqueur just before potting up.
4. Remove from the heat and pot into hot, sterilized jars. Seal and, once cooled, add labels.

TOP TIP

Because cherries are low in pectin, it is essential to use jam sugar with added pectin for this recipe to help it set faster. This means you can cook it for a shorter time to preserve its vibrant colour and flavour.

DAMSON JAM

Damsons, available in late summer and early autumn, have a unique flavour and give this jam a sweet-and-sour twang.

INGREDIENTS *Makes 2kg/4¹/₂lb*
1kg/2¼lb damsons
1.4 litres/2½ pints water
1kg/2¼lb preserving sugar,
    warmed

METHOD
1. Wash the damsons and remove the stalks. There's no need to remove the stones – just place the damsons in the preserving pan with the water and simmer gently until soft. Then press the damsons against the side of the pan to break them open. Now remove the stones from the pan.
2. Add the sugar and stir continuously until it has dissolved completely.
3. Bring the jam to the boil and cook rapidly for about 10 minutes or until the jam sets when tested, removing any stones you have missed as they rise to the surface. Carefully scrape any scum from the jam with a slotted spoon.
4. Pot into hot, sterilized jars. Seal, then label when cool.

DAMSON CHEESE

A simple variation on the damson jam recipe given here is damson cheese. Simmer the fruit and water as described, then rub the fruit through a fine sieve until you have a purée. Add 450g/1lb sugar to each 600ml/1 pint of purée, then follow the recipe as for jam. For more on fruit butters and cheeses, see pages 75–76.

GOOSEBERRY & REDCURRANT JAM

The combination of tart gooseberries and vibrant redcurrants makes this a perfect accompaniment for roast lamb.

INGREDIENTS *Makes 1.35kg/3lb*
750g/1lb 10oz firm gooseberries, topped and tailed
750g/1lb 10oz redcurrants, stalks removed
625ml/21fl oz water
1.5kg/3lb 3oz caster sugar, warmed

METHOD

1. Wash and prepare the fruit, checking that none of the berries is damaged or bruised. Put the fruit into a preserving pan, add the water and simmer over a medium heat for 30 minutes, or until the fruit is soft. Using a potato masher, mash the fruit until it is lightly crushed.
2. Reduce the heat to low, add the sugar and stir continuously until it has dissolved completely.
3. Increase the heat and bring the fruit to the boil. Boil rapidly for 20–30 minutes or until the jam reaches setting point.
4. Remove from the heat, skim off any scum, then leave to stand for 5 minutes before giving it one final stir.
5. Pot up and seal, then leave to cool before labelling.

TOP TIP

The amount of time taken to reach setting point will depend entirely on the ripeness of the gooseberries. The riper the fruit, the longer it will take to reach setting point. This is because unripe fruit contains more pectin than ripe fruit.

GREENGAGE JAM

Greengages make a superb jam. As they are very high in pectin, this preserve will reach setting point quickly.

INGREDIENTS *Makes 2kg/4¹/₂lb*
1.5kg/3lb 3oz firm greengages
250ml/8fl oz water
2 vanilla pods
1.5kg/3lb 3oz preserving sugar, warmed
15g/½oz unsalted butter

METHOD

1. Wash and check over the greengages to make sure they are not bruised or overripe. There is no need to remove the stones as they will rise to the top when the mixture boils, so can be skimmed off easily.

2. Place the fruit in a preserving pan with the water and vanilla pods. Simmer gently for 30 minutes or until the greengages are extremely soft.

3. Turn down the heat and add the sugar, stirring constantly until it has completely dissolved.

4. Increase the heat, add the butter and bring the mixture to the boil. Allow it to boil rapidly for 10 minutes. Use a slotted spoon to remove the stones as they rise, being careful not to burn your hands. Remove the vanilla pods and any scum on the surface and then test for setting point.

5. When the jam is ready, transfer it to hot, sterilized jars, seal tightly and leave to cool before labelling and storing.

LOGANBERRY CONSERVE

This recipe has just two ingredients, so it couldn't be easier to make. Not only is it delicious on hot buttered toast, it also makes a wonderful filling for pies, tarts and crumbles.

INGREDIENTS *Makes 1.35kg/3lb*
1.35kg/3lb loganberries
1.35kg/3lb preserving sugar

METHOD

1. Wash the loganberries and remove any stalks. Make alternate layers of the loganberries and sugar in a large bowl. Cover the bowl with a clean tea towel and leave for 24 hours so that the sugar can draw the natural moisture out of the fruit.

2. Place the fruit and sugar mixture and all the juices in a preserving pan and bring to the boil. Stir the mixture constantly until the sugar has completely dissolved. Boil rapidly for a further 5 minutes.

3. Put the mixture into a large, glass bowl, cover with a clean tea towel and leave in a cool place for 48 hours.

4. Return the fruit to the preserving pan, bring to the boil, stirring from time to time, and boil rapidly for 10 minutes until setting point is reached.

5. Remove from the heat and leave to cool for 15 minutes. Ladle into hot, sterilized jars, cover and seal. Label once the jars have cooled down.

VARIATION

Follow the recipe for loganberry conserve, but substitute raspberries for loganberries.

MARROW & GINGER JAM

Marrow and ginger jam is a traditional recipe, given here with
the addition of cooking apples for extra pectin
to aid the setting process.

INGREDIENTS *Makes 1.8kg/4lb*

1.35kg/3lb vegetable marrow,
  peeled, seeded and chopped
  into cubes
450g/1lb cooking apples, peeled,
  cored and diced
1 tbsp water
2 lemons
60g/2oz fresh root ginger
1.35kg/3lb preserving sugar,
  warmed

METHOD

1. Prepare the marrow and apple
and place in a preserving pan
with the water. Simmer until the
fruit is soft and then mash, using
a potato masher, until you have
a rough pulp.

2. Remove the zest from the
lemons and squeeze out the
juice, retaining the pips.

3. Bruise the root ginger by
hitting it gently with a rolling pin
and then tie it into a square of
muslin along with the lemon
zest and pips. Close the bag
securely with a piece of string
and tie it to the inside of the
preserving pan.

4. Add the lemon juice to the fruit
pulp in the pan. Add the sugar
and bring the fruit to simmering
point, stirring continuously
until the sugar has dissolved
completely.

5. Turn up the heat and boil
rapidly for about 30 minutes,
stirring occasionally as the pulp
starts to thicken. Continue to
cook until setting point is
reached.

6. Ladle the jam into hot,
sterilized jars, seal immediately
and wait for the jam to cool down
before labelling.

MELON & LIME CONSERVE

The delicate flavour of honeydew melon is complemented
by the addition of lime, ginger and star anise.

INGREDIENTS *Makes 2.25kg/5lb*
1.8kg/4lb honeydew melon,
 seeded, peeled and diced
1.8kg/4lb preserving sugar,
 warmed
30g/1oz fresh root ginger
the zest and juice of 3 limes
2 star anise
15g/½oz unsalted butter

METHOD

1. Prepare the melon, put it into
a large glass bowl, sprinkle with
about 450g/1lb of the sugar and
leave to stand overnight. The
sugar will help to draw
out the natural
juices from the
fruit.
2. Bruise the
ginger by hitting
it gently with a
rolling pin to release the
flavour and tie it inside a square
of clean muslin along with the
zest from the limes and the star
anise. Tie the bag with a piece
of string and hang inside the
preserving pan.

3. Put the melon into the pan, add
the lime juice and simmer gently
for 30 minutes.

4. Remove the pan from the heat,
add the remaining sugar and stir
until it has dissolved completely.

5. Add the butter and put the
pan back on the heat. Bring
the mixture to a gentle boil and
simmer for 30 minutes or until
setting point is reached.

6. Take the pan off the heat and
remove the muslin bag. Using
a slotted spoon, remove any
scum that has settled on the
surface and then pot the jam
immediately in hot, sterilized
jars. Seal and leave to cool
before labelling.

PEACH CONSERVE WITH BRANDY

This combination of flavours is a real treat to the taste buds and makes this conserve a wonderful Christmas present.

INGREDIENTS *Makes 2.25kg/5lb*

1.35kg/3lb ripe peaches, skinned, stoned and chopped

115g/4oz slivered almonds

85g/3oz glacé cherries, halved

1 tsp finely grated lemon zest

2 tbsp lemon juice

½ tsp ground cinnamon

1.1kg/2½lb preserving sugar, warmed

5 tbsp brandy

300ml/10fl oz pectin stock (see page 22)

METHOD

1. Prepare the peaches, making sure you collect all the juice. Crack the peach stones with a nutcracker or hammer, take out the kernels and tie them in a piece of clean muslin.

2. Put the fruit into a preserving pan with the muslin bag, the almonds, cherries, lemon zest and juice and cinnamon.

3. Add the sugar and bring to the boil, stirring constantly until the sugar has dissolved completely.

4. Remove the pan from the heat and stir in the brandy and stock.

5. Leave to cool slightly for 5 minutes, then stir again.

6. Pour into hot, sterilized jars and seal immediately. Allow the jars to cool down before labelling and storing.

PEAR & VANILLA JAM

In this jam, vanilla gives an aromatic lift to the subtle flavour of the pears. The preserve goes brilliantly with cheese.

INGREDIENTS *Makes 1.35kg/3lb*
1kg/2½lb pears, peeled, cored
    and chopped
the juice of 3 lemons
300ml/10fl oz water
1 vanilla pod, split
about 700g/1½lb preserving
    sugar, warmed

METHOD

1. Prepare the pears and place them in a preserving pan with the lemon juice, water and split vanilla pod. Bring to the boil, then cover and simmer for 10 minutes.

2. Uncover the pan and continue to cook for a further 15–20 minutes, or until the fruit is soft.

3. Remove the vanilla pod, scrape out the seeds and return them to the pan.

4. Put the pear mixture into a food processor and whizz until you have a fine purée. Carefully measure the purée and return to the preserving pan. For every 600ml/1 pint of purée, add 275g/9½oz warmed sugar.

5. Cook over a medium heat, stirring constantly until the sugar has completely dissolved. Increase the heat and boil rapidly for 15–20 minutes, stirring occasionally, until the mixture forms a thick purée that holds its shape when spooned onto a cold plate. This recipe will not be quite as thick as regular jam.

6. Spoon the jam into hot, sterilized jars and seal immediately. Label once the jars are cool and store in a cool, dark place for at least 5 days before serving.

PINEAPPLE JAM

This jam is delicious served on toasted muffins or crumpets and has a distinctly tropical flavour all of its own.

INGREDIENTS *Makes 250g/9oz*
1 very ripe pineapple, producing
    around 250g/9oz flesh
120ml/4fl oz water
juice of 1 lemon
125g/4½oz preserving sugar,
    warmed

METHOD

1. Peel the pineapple, removing all the brown eyes. Cut out the core and set aside. Chop the flesh into small pieces.

2. Put the pineapple flesh (including the core) in a preserving pan with the water and lemon juice and cook on a low heat for about 30 minutes or until the flesh is very soft.

3. Remove the pineapple core, add the sugar and stir until it is completely dissolved.

4. Increase the heat and bring the mixture to a rolling boil. Cook for about 15 minutes or until the fruit is clear and the jam has reached setting point.

5. Ladle into hot, sterilized jars and seal immediately. Leave to cool before labelling and storing.

POMEGRANATE JAM

Although this jam requires a little effort, the amazing flavour and colour mean that it is well worth it.

INGREDIENTS *Makes 1.35kg/3lb*
8 pomegranates
120ml/4fl oz freshly squeezed
    orange juice
300g/10oz granulated sugar,
    warmed
the juice of a lemon
the zest of an orange

METHOD
1. Extract the seeds from the pomegranates, setting aside the seeds from one fruit. Press the remaining seeds in a fine nylon sieve to extract all the juice. Don't be tempted to use a juicer, as it will make the juice taste bitter. Make sure there is no white membrane mixed in with the seeds as this again will impart a bitter taste.
2. Combine the pomegranate juice, orange juice and sugar in a preserving pan and cook over a medium heat, stirring frequently, until all the sugar has dissolved.
3. Turn the heat to low and continue cooking for a further 60–90 minutes. It is important to keep the heat low, as the jam may turn brown if cooked at too high a heat.
4. Once the jam has taken on the consistency of a thick syrup, add the reserved pomegranate seeds and the lemon juice and cook for another 5–10 minutes over a low heat. Test for setting point. When the jam is ready, add the orange zest and stir.
5. Pot the jam into hot, sterilized jars and seal immediately. Label and store once the jars have cooled.

RASPBERRY JAM

Some people love the flavour of raspberry jam, but don't like the pips. Here's a scrumptious seedless version.

INGREDIENTS *Makes 350g/12oz*
450g/1lb fresh raspberries
450g/1lb preserving sugar,
    warmed, for every
    600ml/1 pint pulp

METHOD
1. Wash the fruit, remove any stalks and discard any damaged or mouldy berries. Put into a preserving pan and gently crush the raspberries on the side of the pan with the back of a wooden

----
TOP TIP

Use a combination of both ripe and under-ripe raspberries to make sure that you obtain a good set on your finished jam.
----

spoon to help release their natural juices. Gently bring the fruit to boiling point, then turn down the heat and simmer for 10 minutes, stirring occasionally, until the fruit is soft.
2. Pour the mixture into a fine nylon sieve over a bowl and, using the back of a wooden spoon, gently push the purée through until only the pips are left. Discard the pips and measure the amount of fruit pulp before returning it to the pan.
3. For every 600ml/1 pint of pulp add 450g/1lb sugar. Return the pan to the heat and cook gently, stirring, until the sugar dissolves. Increase the heat and boil rapidly for 10–15 minutes or until setting point is reached.
4. Skim off any froth with a slotted spoon, then ladle the jam into hot, sterilized jars and seal.

REDCURRANT & RASPBERRY JAM

The vibrant red colour of these summer fruits makes this the perfect
jam to go with the typical English tea of scones and cream.

INGREDIENTS *Makes 1.8kg/4lb*
1.8kg/4lb raspberries, stalks
   removed
200ml/7fl oz water
2.25kg/5lb preserving sugar,
   warmed
225g/8oz redcurrants, stalks
   removed

METHOD
1. Put the raspberries into a
preserving pan with the water.
Cook over a low heat until they
start to lose a little of their juice.

2. Add the sugar and cook
over a medium heat, stirring
all the time, until the sugar has
dissolved.
3. Turn up the heat and, when the
raspberries have broken down
and the mixture is boiling, add
the redcurrants. Boil for a further
10–15 minutes or until the jam
has reached setting point.
4. Pot up the jam into hot,
sterilized jars and seal
immediately. Leave to cool before
labelling and storing.

RHUBARB JAM

This is the rhubarb lover's delight, as the jam retains the tartness of the fruit and is a wonderful pink colour.

INGREDIENTS *Makes 550g/1¹/4lb*
450g/1lb fresh rhubarb
the juice and finely grated zest of
   1 orange
450g/1lb preserving sugar,
   warmed

METHOD

1. Wash the rhubarb and remove any stringy parts. Pat dry and slice into 2.5cm/1in pieces. Check the weight of the fruit after it has been prepared to make sure you have the correct amount.

2. Put the rhubarb and orange zest and juice into a preserving pan and cover with the sugar. Place over a gentle heat and stir continuously to prevent burning until the sugar has completely dissolved.

3. Once the sugar has dissolved, turn up the heat and boil the jam for 10 minutes, then remove the pan from the heat. Test for setting point. If it is not quite ready, return the pan to the heat for another 3–4 minutes and test again. If you are happy that the jam is set, remove from the heat.

4. Ladle the jam into hot, sterilized jars and seal immediately with lids. Allow the jars to cool before labelling and storing.

TOP TIP

Young shoots of rhubarb are not suitable for making jam as their flavour is too delicate; wait until later in the season when the stalks have matured.

RHUBARB & STRAWBERRY JAM

This combination of flavours will set your taste buds tingling. The jam very easy to make and is great used as a pie or tart filling.

INGREDIENTS *Makes 2.25kg/5lb*
500g/1lb 2oz fresh rhubarb
700g/1½lb strawberries, sliced
2 tbsp lemon juice
15g/½oz unsalted butter
2kg/4½lb preserving sugar,
    warmed

METHOD
1. Wash the rhubarb and remove any stringy parts. Pat dry and slice into 2.5cm/1in pieces. Prepare the strawberries and then add the fruit to a preserving pan with the lemon juice and butter. Cook over a medium heat, stirring from time to time, until the fruit is soft and the natural juices have started to come out.
2. Add the sugar about 200g/7oz at a time, and stir continuously until it has dissolved.
3. Increase the heat and bring the mixture to a rolling boil. Cook and stir for 1–2 minutes. Remove from the heat and skim off any foam that has formed. Test for setting point and cook for a further 2 minutes if necessary.
4. Ladle the jam into hot, sterilized jars, making sure you fill them right to the top. Seal with lids straight away and avoid moving the jars until they have cooled to help the jam set.

ROLLING BOIL

The phrase 'rolling boil' refers to a liquid that is boiling rapidly with lots of bubbling. Jam should be boiling so vigorously that stirring it doesn't stop the bubbling.

SUMMER BERRY JAM

Once the blackberries are ripe in the hedgerows, try combining them with other summer fruits to make this fragrant jam.

INGREDIENTS *Makes 1.8kg/4lb*
1.8kg/4lb mixed berries
   (strawberries, raspberries,
   redcurrants, blackcurrants and
   blackberries)
1.5kg/3lb 3oz jam sugar
the juice and pips of 1 lemon
15g/½oz unsalted butter

METHOD

1. The day before you want to make your jam, wash the fruit, remove any stalks and layer the berries and sugar in a large bowl. Cover with cling film and leave to rest overnight at room temperature.

2. Put the fruit and sugar mixture into a preserving pan and stir in the lemon juice. Collect the pips when squeezing the lemons, tie them securely in a piece of clean muslin and add to the pan. Cook the mixture over a low heat until the sugar has completely dissolved, stirring from time to time.

3. Increase the heat and boil the jam for 5 minutes. Remove from the heat and test for setting point. If it is not ready, return to the heat for 2–3 minutes at a time until you have the desired consistency.

4. Remove from the heat, skim off any scum, take out the muslin bag, then stir in the butter to dissolve any remaining scum. Leave the jam to stand for 10 minutes before potting up into hot, sterilized jars.

- - - - - - - - - - - - - - - - -

TOP TIP

Cooking the lemon pips extracts their pectin content.

- - - - - - - - - - - - - - - - -

STRAWBERRY CONSERVE

You must not rush when making strawberry conserve, so make sure you have plenty of time for the preparation stages.

INGREDIENTS *Makes 1.35kg/3lb*
1.35kg/3lb medium-sized
    strawberries, washed
    and hulled
1.35kg/3lb granulated sugar

METHOD

1. Wash and dry the strawberries and layer them with the sugar in a large bowl. Cover the bowl with cling film and leave to rest for 24 hours at room temperature.

2. Transfer the strawberries, sugar and juice to a preserving pan. Heat gently, stirring occasionally, until all the sugar has dissolved.

3. Turn up the heat and bring to a rolling boil for 5 minutes.

4. Remove the pan from the heat and allow the mixture to cool. Transfer the jam to a bowl, cover with cling film and leave to chill in the refrigerator for 2 days.

5. Put the jam back into a clean preserving pan and bring to the boil. Cook steadily for 10 minutes, then remove from the heat and leave to stand for a further 10 minutes.

6. Pour into hot, sterilized jars and seal. Label when cool.

TOP TIP

Once you have washed fruit, use it straight away as it will quickly lose its freshness if left to stand.

STRAWBERRY & KIWI JAM

This is a truly inspirational combination of flavours that is so mouth-watering it's hard to resist a second or third helping.

INGREDIENTS *Makes 900g/2lb*
750g/1lb 10oz strawberries,
    washed, hulled and halved
250g/9oz kiwi fruit, peeled and
    diced
the grated zest of 1 lemon
1kg/2¼lb jam sugar, warmed

- - - - - - - - - - - - - - - - -
TOP TIP

Here is a quick and easy way to peel kiwi fruit. Cut off both ends of the kiwi, then slip a teaspoon under the skin and follow the fruit's natural curve. Slide the spoon around the kiwi to separate the flesh from the skin. Once you get the hang of it the flesh will come out in one piece.
- - - - - - - - - - - - - - - - -

METHOD

1. Prepare the strawberries and kiwi fruit. Put all the fruit and lemon zest into a preserving pan and heat until it reaches boiling point, stirring occasionally.

2. Boil for 1 minute, then gradually add the sugar, stirring continuously, until it has dissolved completely. Bring the jam back to the boil and cook for a further 3 minutes.

3. Remove from the heat and stir for a minute to mix in any foam on the surface. Check for set and continue cooking for another couple of minutes if the mixture is still too runny.

4. Ladle the jam into hot, sterilized jars, put on the lids, then stand the jars upside down for 5 minutes to make sure the fruit is evenly distributed throughout the jam.

SWEET CHILLI JAM

This preserve has quite a kick and goes extremely well with cold meats and cheese.

INGREDIENTS *Makes 1kg/2¼lb*

8 red peppers, deseeded
  and chopped
5 medium red chillies (including
  seeds), roughly chopped
5cm/2in fresh root ginger, peeled
  and roughly chopped
8 garlic cloves, chopped
400g/14oz tomatoes, skinned and
  roughly chopped
750g/1lb 10oz caster sugar
250ml/8fl oz red wine vinegar

METHOD

1. Put the peppers, chillies, ginger and garlic into a food processor and whizz until they are finely chopped.
2. Put the pepper mixture into a preserving pan and add the tomatoes, sugar and vinegar. Bring to the boil.
3. With a slotted spoon, skim off any scum that has formed on the surface, then turn down the heat to simmering point. Cook for about 50 minutes, stirring occasionally.
4. After the jam starts to thicken, continue cooking for a further 10–15 minutes, stirring frequently so that it doesn't stick to the bottom of the pan.
5. When the jam has really thickened, take it off the heat and cool slightly before transferring to hot, sterilized jars.

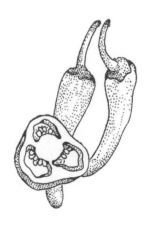

TOMATO, APPLE & ROSEMARY JAM

This jam is so delicious you'll find it hard not to eat it straight out of the jar. If you can wait, it goes well with roast duck or goose.

INGREDIENTS *Makes 675g/1¹/₂lb*
500g/1lb 2oz tomatoes, skinned and roughly chopped
400g/14oz cooking apples, peeled, cored and roughly chopped
the juice of 2 lemons
550g/1¹/₄lb preserving sugar
2 sprigs of fresh rosemary

METHOD
1. Prepare the tomatoes, discarding any excess juice and seeds. Put the tomato flesh into a preserving pan.
2. Prepare the apples and place in the preserving pan. Add the lemon juice and toss the tomatoes and apples until they are completely covered.
3. Add the sugar and the sprigs of rosemary. Put the pan over a medium heat and bring up to a gentle boil, stirring gently to

make sure that all the sugar has dissolved.
4. Pour the contents into a large glass bowl, cover with cling film and leave to stand in the refrigerator overnight.
5. The next day, transfer the ingredients back into the clean preserving pan. Remove the rosemary and skim off any foam. Bring to a boil and continue to cook until the apples are translucent. Use a slotted spoon to remove the tomato and apple pieces and set aside.
6. Cook the remaining syrup until it reaches 105°C/220°F. Return the apple and tomato flesh to the pan and bring back to the boil. Skim off any scum and cook until the jam reaches 105°C/220°F.
7. Ladle into hot, sterilized jars, seal with lids and turn upside down until completely cool.

VICTORIA PLUM & CLEMENTINE JAM

The depth of flavour of the Victoria plums is heightened by the addition of the zest and juice from fresh-tasting clementines.

INGREDIENTS *Makes 1kg/2¼lb*
1.5kg/3lb 3oz Victoria plums
the juice and finely grated zest of
  2 clementines
1.5kg/3lb 3oz preserving sugar,
  warmed

METHOD
1. Prepare the plums by removing the stones and roughly chopping the flesh. Put the flesh into a preserving pan.
2. Add the clementine zest and juice to the preserving pan.
3. Heat gently and cook until the plums are pulpy and well cooked, stirring occasionally.
4. Add the sugar and slowly increase the heat, stirring well to make sure that all the sugar has dissolved before the jam reaches boiling point.
5. Once the jam has reached boiling point, continue to cook at a rolling boil for 20 minutes or until setting point is reached.
6. Remove from the heat and transfer to hot, sterilized jars. Seal and leave to cool before putting on labels and storing.

VICTORIA PLUMS

As the name suggests, this plum variety dates back to the Victorian era, although little is known of its origin. It has long been the culinary plum of choice as its flavour is unparalled and its flesh cooks to a distinctive pink-orange colour. It makes a superior jam and a wonderful filling for pies, crumbles and puddings.

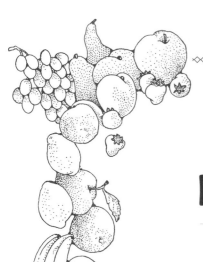

PART 3

JELLIES

Unlike jams and conserves, jellies are clear and made from the juice of cooked fruit. The basic principles are the same as for making jam, with the same ingredients – sugar, acid and pectin – needed to make the jelly set, but you will need considerably more fruit. Only distinctively flavoured fruits are suitable for making jellies and those that are low in pectin will need to be combined with high-pectin fruit to get the correct consistency of set.

MAKING JELLIES

To make the perfect jelly, all traces of pulp, skin and seed must be removed, so you will need one more piece of equipment than is required for jam – a jelly bag.

For your first attempt, you can improvise your own jelly bag if you don't want to buy one (see page 17). However, if you find that you enjoy making jelly and plan to do it regularly it's worth buying a jelly bag for the sake of convenience – they are not expensive and can easily be acquired from online stores if you can't find one in a local shop. Just like the jars used in making jam, the jelly bag must be made sterile by scalding in boiling water before each use.

The best types of fruit for making jellies are those with a strong flavour such as crab apples, cooking apples, blackberries, blackcurrants, gooseberries, loganberries and redcurrants. As in the case of jam making, they must all be really fresh and undamaged or your jelly won't be a success.

To prepare the fruit you need to check it over carefully for any signs of bruising or decay. There is no need to peel, core or remove stalks or stones, as the fruit will be strained during the cooking process. How long this takes will depend on the type of fruit used – some may take just 2–3 hours to release all their juice while others will need as long as 12 hours to drain completely.

Once the fruit has finished draining, you will need to measure the amount of liquid accurately and continue as you would for making jam, following the recipe carefully. The best way to test for setting point is to use the flake method (see page 24) or a sugar thermometer.

TIPS FOR MAKING JELLIES

• Although it's not necessary to remove the peel or stones when you prepare fruit for jellies, it is advisable to cut the larger types of fruit such as apples into fairly small pieces in order to reduce the cooking time. Cooking for a shorter time will ensure a fresh, intense flavour.

• Simmer the fruit gently to extract as much pectin as possible.

• If you are cooking hard fruit that takes a long time to soften, cover the pan so that you don't lose too much liquid and remove the lid halfway through the cooking time.

• Jellies need to be potted immediately as they start to set very quickly. Make sure the jelly and jars are hot before you start potting up.

• If you find the jelly starts setting in the pan, put it back on the heat briefly until it becomes liquid again.

• As you put the jelly into the jars, gently tap the side of the glass to try to remove any air bubbles. Alternatively, to fill the jars, tip the jar at an angle and gently pour in the jelly against the side.

• If you find you have a lot of scum on the surface of the jelly, drain it through a piece of sterilized muslin before potting. Don't add butter as suggested for jam as this will make your jelly cloudy.

• Resist the temptation to squeeze the pulp in the jelly bag to extract the juice as this will also result in cloudy jelly.

• Avoid disturbing the jars until the jelly is completely set.

• Use leftover fruit pulp to make fruit cheeses (see pages 75–6 for details).

APPLE & PLUM JELLY

Damsons or dark red plums give this jelly a rich ruby colour and
make it a lovely accompaniment to roast lamb.

INGREDIENTS *Makes 1kg/2¼lb*
900g/2lb damsons or dark
    red plums
450g/1lb cooking apples such
    as Bramley
1 cinnamon stick
750ml/1¼ pints water
450g/1lb preserving sugar for
    every 600ml/1 pint liquid

METHOD
1. Cut the damsons or plums
in half and remove the stones.
Roughly chop the flesh. Chop
the apples into small pieces,
including the peel and core. Put
all the fruit into a preserving pan
with the cinnamon stick.
2. Bring the mixture to the boil
then reduce to a simmer. Cover
the pan and cook gently for 30
minutes or until the fruit is soft
and pulpy.
3. Pour the fruit pulp into a jelly

bag suspended over a large
bowl and leave to drain for
about 3 hours, or until it has
stopped dripping.
4. Measure the quantity of liquid
from the strained fruit and put
it back into the preserving pan.
Add the sugar.
5. Bring the mixture to a boil,
stirring occasionally until the
sugar has dissolved completely.
Increase the heat and boil
rapidly for about 10 minutes or
until the jelly reaches setting
point (105°C/220°F on a sugar
thermometer). Once it is the
correct temperature, remove
the pan from the heat.
6. Remove any scum from the
surface with a slotted spoon, then
immediately pour the jelly into
hot, sterilized jars. Cover and
seal while the jelly is still hot.
Wait to cool before labelling.

APPLE & QUINCE JELLY

The lovely floral flavour of quince comes through in this jelly, balanced perfectly by the tartness of the apples.

INGREDIENTS *Makes 900g/2lb*
675g/1½lb ripe quince, chopped
   into small pieces
900g/2lb cooking apples,
   chopped into small pieces
450g/1lb preserving sugar for
   every 600ml/1 pint liquid
the juice of 1 lemon
2 vanilla pods, split lengthwise

METHOD
1. Wash and prepare the quince and place in a large pan with just enough water to cover. Bring to the boil, then turn down the heat and simmer for about 2 hours or until the fruit is soft and starting to turn pink.
2. Wash and prepare the apples. Place in a separate pan with just enough water to cover and bring to the boil over a medium heat. Lower the heat and then simmer for about 30 minutes or until the apples are soft.
3. Put the cooked apples and quince into a jelly bag over a large bowl and leave for several hours (or overnight) to drain.
4. Measure the juice carefully and return to a clean preserving pan with the correct amount of sugar as given in the ingredients. Add the lemon juice and vanilla pods and bring to the boil, stirring continuously until the sugar has dissolved.
5. Continue to boil rapidly, skimming the surface from time to time to remove the scum. When the jelly reaches setting point (105°C/220°F), boil for 1 minute, then remove from the heat.
6. Remove the vanilla pods, cut into 5cm/2in pieces and put 2–3 pieces in each jar. Ladle the jelly into hot, sterilized jars.

BLACKBERRY & SLOE GIN JELLY

This hedgerow recipe uses autumn fruits to produce a rich,
deep purple coloured jelly.

INGREDIENTS *Makes 1.35kg/3lb*
450g/1lb ripe sloes
600ml/1 pint water
1.8kg/4lb ripe blackberries
juice of 1 lemon
450g/1lb preserving sugar for
    every 600ml/1 pint liquid
3 tbsp gin

METHOD

1. Wash the sloes and prick them with a fork in a couple of places. Put them in a large saucepan with the water and bring to the boil. Reduce the heat, cover the pan with a lid and simmer for 5 minutes.

2. Wash the blackberries and put them into a preserving pan with the lemon juice. Add the sloes and any remaining liquid to the pan and simmer gently. Cook for about 20 minutes, or until the fruit is tender, stirring occasionally.

3. Pour the fruit and all the juices into a jelly bag set over a bowl. Leave to drain for at least 4 hours or until the juices have stopped dripping.

4. Measure the liquid carefully, return it to a clean preserving pan, then add the amount of sugar recommended in the ingredients. Heat gently, stirring all the time, until the sugar has dissolved. Increase the heat and boil rapidly for 10 minutes or until the jelly reaches setting point. Remove the pan from the heat, skim off any scum and then stir in the gin.

5. Pour the jelly into hot, sterilized jars, seal and allow to cool before labelling.

This rich jelly goes well with roast meats, and can be stored for 2 years in a cool, dark place.

BLACKCURRANT JELLY

Blackcurrants have plenty of natural pectin and if you use the right amount of sugar this jelly sets a treat.

INGREDIENTS *Makes 900g/2lb*
1.8kg/4lb blackcurrants
1.7 litres/3 pints water
450g/1lb preserving sugar for
    every 600ml/1 pint liquid

METHOD

1. Wash the blackcurrants and drain well. Check that all the fruit is in good condition and discard any soft or bruised blackcurrants.

2. Put the blackcurrants into a preserving pan and add the water. Bring to the boil, then simmer gently for about 25 minutes until the fruit is soft and pulpy. Crush the fruit gently against the side of the pan to release all its flavour.

3. Put the fruit pulp into a jelly bag and leave to drip for at least 4 hours, or until it is fully drained of all its juices.

4. Measure the juice carefully, then pour it back into a clean preserving pan.

5. Add sugar as recommended in the ingredients, then bring to the boil, stirring until the sugar has completely dissolved. Cook at a rolling boil for 25–30 minutes, skimming off any foam from time to time. After 20 minutes, keep checking the jelly for setting point.

6. When it is ready, pour the jelly into hot, sterilized jars, seal and leave to cool before labelling.

TOP TIP

When picking blackcurrants, run the teeth of an ordinary kitchen fork down the stalk – you will find it much quicker.

BRAMBLE JELLY

Bramble jelly is one of the most delectable of all the jelly recipes and costs little because you pick most of the fruit for free.

INGREDIENTS *Makes 900g/2lb*
1.35kg/3lb blackberries, washed
2 large cooking apples, washed
    and diced
450ml/15fl oz water
the juice of 1 lemon
450g/1lb preserving sugar to
    every 600ml/1 pint liquid

METHOD
1. Put the blackberries, prepared apples, water and lemon juice into a preserving pan. Bring to the boil, then reduce the heat and simmer gently for 20–25 minutes or until the fruit is completely soft.
2. Put the fruit pulp into a jelly bag and leave to drain for at least 8 hours or until it has stopped dripping.
3. Measure the amount of fruit juice and put into a preserving pan. Add sugar as recommended in the ingredients.
4. Heat the juice over a low heat until all the sugar has dissolved, stirring constantly. Once you are happy it has dissolved, turn up the heat and bring to a boil. Boil rapidly for 10–15 minutes or until setting point is reached.
5. Skim away any scum from the surface and fill hot, sterilized jars right up to the brim. Seal and label once the jars are cool.

TOP TIP

Only pick berries that are fully black and avoid washing them until you are ready to use them.

CITRUS JELLY

This jelly is really light and fresh and has a lovely citrus tang. If you want a beautiful pink tinge to your jelly, use blood oranges.

INGREDIENTS *Makes 1.35kg/3lb*
900g/2lb oranges
450g/1lb lemons
450g/1lb limes
2 litres/3½ pints water
450g/1lb preserving sugar for
    every 600ml/1 pint liquid
1 sprig of fresh lemon thyme,
    leaves only

METHOD
1. Wash all the fruit and cut up into small pieces, leaving the peel on. Put into a preserving pan with all the pips and pour the water over.
2. Bring the mixture to a boil, then reduce the heat, cover and simmer for 1 hour or until the fruit has gone pulpy.
3. Pour the pulp into a jelly bag over a large bowl and leave to drain for at least 3 hours or until the juices have stopped dripping.

4. Measure the juice carefully and pour into a clean preserving pan. Add sugar in the quantity given in the ingredients. Heat gently, stirring constantly, until the sugar has dissolved completely. Increase the heat and bring to the boil. Boil rapidly for about 10 minutes or until setting point is reached.
5. Remove the pan from the heat and skim off any scum from the surface. Stir the thyme leaves into the jelly. Leave it to stand for a few minutes or until a thin skin forms on the surface. Stir it again gently to make sure the thyme leaves are evenly distributed.
6. Pour into hot, sterilized jars, seal and leave to cool.

For a different flavour, replace the lemons and limes with grapefruit and tangerines.

CRAB APPLE JELLY

Crab apples are often found growing wild in the autumn. They are perfect for jellies as they don't need extra pectin to set.

INGREDIENTS *Makes 900g/2lb*
2kg/4½lb crab apples
450g/1lb preserving sugar for
  every 600ml/1 pint liquid
the juice of 1 lemon

METHOD

1. Wash the crab apples, remove the stalks and cut out any areas that are bruised. Chop the fruit into smaller pieces, then put it in a preserving pan and add sufficient water to cover.

2. Bring the mixture to a boil, then turn down the heat and simmer gently for 25 minutes or until the fruit is soft.

3. Pour the fruit into a jelly bag and leave to drip overnight into a bowl. Don't be tempted to squeeze the jelly bag or your jelly will end up cloudy.

4. Measure the juice carefully and then put into a clean preserving pan with sugar in the quantity given in the ingredients. Add the lemon juice and bring to the boil, stirring continuously, until the sugar has dissolved.

5. Keep the mixture at a rolling boil for 35–40 minutes, skimming off any scum on the surface at regular intervals.

6. Test for set by using the flake method (see page 24).

7. When the jelly is ready, pour into hot, sterilized jars and seal tightly while still warm.

VARIATION

For a spicy version of this jelly add 45g/1½oz of chopped red chilli peppers when cooking the apples.

ELDERBERRY JELLY

Try this wonderfully spicy version of elderberry jelly at Christmas as a delicious alternative to cranberry sauce.

INGREDIENTS *Makes 1.35kg/3lb*
1kg/2¼lb elderberries, prepared weight
1kg/2¼lb cooking apples
450g/1lb preserving sugar to every 600ml/1 pint liquid

FOR THE SPICE BAG:
1 tsp allspice
5 cloves
10cm/4in cinnamon stick
1 star anise
2.5cm/1in fresh root ginger

METHOD
1. Wash the elderberries and then strip them from their stalks using a fork. Wash the cooking apples, then chop including the skin and cores.
2. Put the fruit in a preserving pan and cover with cold water. Bring to the boil, then reduce the heat and simmer gently for about 45 minutes or until the fruit is soft and pulpy.
3. Pour the pulp and juices into a jelly bag over a large bowl and leave to drain overnight.
4. Make up the spice bag using a square of washed muslin. Bruise the whole spices to release their flavours then put them all into the muslin and tie firmly with a piece of string.
5. Measure the juice and place in a pan with the spice bag and sugar in the quantity given in the ingredients. Heat gently, stirring, until the sugar has dissolved. Then increase the heat and boil rapidly until setting point is reached.
6. Remove the spice bag and pour the jelly into hot, sterilized jars. Seal them immediately and then leave to cool before labelling and storing.

GRAPE JELLY

This is a wonderfully vibrant red when finished and can be used as a spread or an accompaniment to dark meat.

INGREDIENTS *Makes 900g/2lb*
1kg/2¼lb red grapes with seeds,
   left whole
450g/1lb preserving sugar to
   every 600ml/1 pint liquid
the juice of 1 lemon

METHOD
1. Wash the grapes and put them into a preserving pan. Cook the grapes gently, covered, for 5–10 minutes or until the juices start to run.
2. Take a potato masher and press the grapes to the sides of the pan to break them up and release their juices. Leave to cook for a further 10 minutes, mashing every now and again until they start to fall apart.
3. Pour the grape mixture into a jelly bag set over a large bowl and then leave the mixture to drain for several hours or overnight until the juices stop dripping.
4. Measure out the juice and pour it into a clean preserving pan with sufficient sugar as recommended in the ingredients. Stir in the lemon juice. Heat gently, stirring continuously until the sugar has dissolved.
5. Turn up the heat and allow the mixture to boil rapidly, skimming off any scum that appears. Continue cooking until the mixture reaches 105°C/220°F on a sugar thermometer.
6. When setting point is reached, remove from the heat, pour into hot, sterilized jars and seal immediately.

For an aromatic flavour, add 1 tablespoon of white cardamom pods when cooking the grapes in step 1.

MINT & APPLE JELLY

A wonderfully refreshing combination of apples and mint, this makes a lovely change from mint sauce when serving roast lamb.

INGREDIENTS *Makes 900g/2lb*
1.8kg/4lb cooking apples, cut into small pieces including the peel and cores
1.2 litres/2 pints water
450g/1lb preserving sugar to every 600ml/1 pint liquid
85g/3oz fresh mint, finely chopped

METHOD

1. Prepare the apples and put them into a preserving pan with the water. Bring to the boil, then turn down the heat and cook slowly until the fruit is soft and pulpy.

2. Transfer the pulp and all its juices into a jelly bag suspended over a large bowl and leave overnight to drain.

3. Measure the apple juice carefully and return to a clean preserving pan. Add sugar in the quantity given in the ingredients. Heat the mixture gently, stirring continuously until the sugar has dissolved. Increase the heat and bring to the boil. Add the chopped mint and boil rapidly until the jelly sets when tested.

4. Remove from the heat and pour into hot, sterilized jars. Seal immediately and label when the jars have cooled down.

PEAR & POMEGRANATE JELLY

This jelly has a delicate, perfumed flavour but because pears and pomegranates are not rich in pectin you need to add pectin stock.

INGREDIENTS *Makes 1.1kg/2½lb*
900g/2lb pears
the pared rind and juice of
    2 lemons
1 cinnamon stick
750ml/1¼ pints water
900g/2lb pomegranates
450g/1lb preserving sugar to
    every 600ml/1 pint liquid
250ml/8fl oz pectin stock (see
    page 22)

METHOD

1. Wash the pears, remove the stalks and chop roughly. Put the fruit into a preserving pan with the lemon rind and juice, cinnamon and water. Bring to a boil, then reduce the heat, cover and simmer gently for 15 minutes.

2. While the pears are cooking, cut the pomegranates in half and use a lemon squeezer to extract all the juice.

3. Add the pomegranate juice to the pears and bring the mixture back to the boil. Reduce the heat and simmer for a further 2 minutes.

4. Pour the pear mixture into a jelly bag set over a large bowl and leave to drain for at least 3 hours.

5. Measure the strained juice carefully and put into a preserving pan with the quantity of sugar given in the ingredients. Heat gently, stirring from time to time, until the sugar has dissolved. Increase the heat and boil rapidly for 3 minutes.

6. Remove from the heat and immediately stir in the pectin stock.

7. Skim off any scum from the surface and then pour the jelly into hot, sterilized jars. Cover and seal. Use within 18 months.

REDCURRANT JELLY

———— ••••◉••• ————

This recipe is far removed from the sickly-sweet type of jelly you find on supermarket shelves, which seems to have lost the authentic tart flavour of the fruit.

INGREDIENTS *Makes 1.35kg/3lb*
1.35kg/3lb just-ripe redcurrants
600ml/1 pint water
450g/1lb preserving sugar to
   every 600ml/1 pint liquid

METHOD
1. Wash and drain the redcurrants – there's no need to remove them from the stalks but do discard any berries that are bruised or overripe.
2. Put the redcurrants into a preserving pan with the water and simmer gently for 30 minutes, or until the fruit is very soft and pulpy. Stir occasionally during the cooking time, gently pressing the berries against the side of the pan with the back of a wooden spoon.
3. Pour the cooked fruit with the juice into a jelly bag set over a large bowl and leave for at least 4 hours or until the juice stops dripping. Do not squeeze or press the fruit at this stage or your final jelly will not be clear.
4. Measure the liquid carefully and test the pectin levels. If the level is low, add a little lemon juice to aid with setting. Return the juice to a clean preserving pan and add sugar in the quantity given in the ingredients.
5. Heat the mixture gently, stirring frequently, until the sugar has dissolved completely. Increase the heat and then boil rapidly for about 10 minutes or until setting point has been reached.
6. Remove the pan from the heat and skim any froth from the surface using a slotted spoon. Pot the jelly immediately into hot, sterilized jars as it will set quickly.

ROSE HIP & APPLE JELLY

A delicious jelly rich in vitamin C, this can be made inexpensively using windfalls and wild rose hips.

INGREDIENTS *Makes 1.8kg/4lb*
1kg/2¼lb cooking apples
300ml/10fl oz water, plus extra
   to cover fruit
450g/1lb firm ripe rose hips
450g/1lb preserving sugar to
   every 600ml/1 pint liquid

METHOD

1. Wash and chop the apples including the peel and cores. If you are using windfalls, make sure you cut out any bruised areas as they will taint the flavour of the jelly.

2. Place the prepared apples in a preserving pan and pour in just enough water to cover the fruit, plus an extra 300ml/10 fl oz. Bring the mixture to a boil, reduce the heat and cook gently until the apples soften and start to go pulpy.

3. Chop the rose hips or whizz them in a mini food processor until they are in fairly large pieces. Add the rose hips and all their pips to the pan and simmer for a further 10 minutes.

4. Remove the pan from the heat and leave to cool for 10 minutes.

5. Pour the pulp into a jelly bag suspended over a large bowl and drain for several hours, or overnight.

6. Measure the juice carefully and pour into a clean preserving pan. Bring to the boil, then add sugar in the quantity given in the ingredients. Cook gently, stirring, until all the sugar has dissolved. Increase the heat and then boil until the jelly reads 105°C/220°F on a sugar thermometer or has reached setting point.

7. Pour immediately into hot, sterilized jars and seal.

SLOE & APPLE JELLY

This jelly has a good depth of flavour and is perfect with red meat or game such as venison or pheasant.

INGREDIENTS *Makes 900g/2lb*
675g/1½lb cooking apples
675g/1½lb sloes
the peel and juice of 1 lemon
450g/1lb preserving sugar to
    every 600ml/1 pint liquid

METHOD

1. Wash the apples and roughly chop them, including the skins and cores. If you are using windfalls, cut out and discard any bad or bruised parts.

2. Wash the sloes and prick them with a fork.

3. Place the apples and sloes in a preserving pan with the peel and juice of the lemon and just enough water to cover the fruit. Bring slowly to the boil, then turn down the heat and simmer gently for about 20–25 minutes or until the fruit is soft and pulpy. Squash the sloes against the side of the pan with the back of a wooden spoon to help extract as much juice as possible.

4. Pour the fruit and liquid into a jelly bag over a large bowl and leave to drain overnight.

5. Measure the strained juice and return it to a clean preserving pan. Add sugar in the quantity given in the ingredients.

6. Heat the mixture, stirring gently and continuously, until the sugar has dissolved. Increase the heat, bring to a rapid boil and cook for 10 minutes before testing for set.

7. Skim off any foam from the surface with a slotted spoon, then pour the jelly into hot, sterilized jars. Seal immediately, then label and store when cold.

TOMATO & CHILLI JELLY

Tomato jelly infused with spicy chillies is a perfect condiment
for a cheese platter and for spicing up pasta sauces.

INGREDIENTS *Makes 1.35kg/3lb*
1.35kg/3lb tomatoes, halved
3 lemons, roughly chopped
2 red chillies, 1 roughly chopped,
   1 thinly sliced, seeds removed
450ml/15fl oz water
450g/1lb preserving sugar for
   every 600ml/1 pint liquid
1 green chilli, thinly sliced with
   seeds removed
60g/2oz fresh herbs such as
   parsley, rosemary and thyme,
   finely chopped

METHOD
1. Put the tomatoes, lemons,
chopped red chilli and water into
a preserving pan. Bring to the
boil, then reduce the heat and
cover with a lid or large sheet of
foil and simmer for 40 minutes.
2. Leave the mixture to cool
slightly, then pour into a jelly bag
suspended over a large bowl.

Leave to drain overnight.
3. Measure the juice and return
it to a clean preserving pan. Add
sugar in the quantity given in
the ingredients. Heat the mixture
gently until the sugar has
dissolved, stirring from time to
time. Increase the heat and bring
to the boil. Stir in the sliced red
and green chillies and chopped
herbs and cook on a rolling boil
for 20–30 minutes or until setting
point is reached.
4. Skim off any scum that has
collected on the surface with
a slotted spoon. Leave the jelly
to stand for 15 minutes then give
it one final stir to make sure the
chillies and herbs are evenly
distributed.
5. Pour into hot, sterilized jars
and seal. Label and store once
cool. This jelly will keep for
6 months.

MAKING FRUIT BUTTERS & CHEESES

Fruit butters and cheeses were once an indispensable item on Victorian and Edwardian tea tables. They were often used in place of dairy cheese and as an accompaniment to bread and butter or a filling for cakes and trifles.

The fruit pulp left over from making jellies is perfect for turning into fruit cheeses and butters. You need the same equipment as for making jam, with the addition of a fine nylon or plastic sieve (metal is not suitable) to get rid of any skin or pips that are left after straining.

Fruit butters are smoother and thicker than jam and can be spread in much the same way as dairy butter. Fruit cheeses are much stiffer and can be cut into slices or wedges, like their dairy counterparts.

To use up any of the fruit pulps left over from the recipes in the Jellies section, follow these instructions:

1. For both butters and cheeses, pour enough hot water into the pulp to make a soft purée and then rub it through a fine nylon or plastic sieve. Weigh the sieved purée and put it into a clean preserving pan.

2. To make fruit butter, boil the fruit and water purée until it is thick, then stir in half the weight of sugar to purée. Simmer gently until the mixture is thick and creamy. The butter is ready when no liquid is visible and the surface appears creamy. You can treat fruit butter much the same as jam, by storing it in hot, sterilized jars and sealing immediately. It does not keep well and only has a storage life of a few weeks. Once opened, a fruit butter will need to be eaten within a few days.

3. To make a fruit cheese, add sugar to the same weight as the fruit pulp. Heat gently and stir until all the sugar has dissolved. Simmer for 1 hour or until the cheese thickens, stirring occasionally, then transfer to a container. Fruit cheese is usually made in a mould, so choose a bowl, wide-necked jar or mould and coat the inside with oil or glycerine so that you can turn out the cheese easily. A fruit cheese will benefit from being left to mature for a couple of weeks before using.

APPLE CIDER CHEESE

You can use leftover apple pulp for the following recipe, or you can start from scratch.

INGREDIENTS

Makes approx 250g/9oz
500g/1lb 2oz cooking apples,
    roughly chopped
200ml/7fl oz dry cider

5 cloves
about 500g/1lb 2oz sugar

METHOD

1. Wash and roughly chop the apples including the skins and cores. Put in a preserving pan with the cider and cloves and bring to the boil. Reduce the heat and simmer gently for 20 minutes or until the fruit is soft and pulpy.

2. Push the pulp through a fine sieve and discard the skin, seeds and cloves. Weigh the purée and then put it back into the pan with an amount of sugar equal to the weight of the pulp. Heat slowly, stirring, until the sugar has dissolved, then increase the heat and cook until the mixture resembles a very thick paste. If you draw a line on the surface and it doesn't close over again, the cheese is ready.

3. Spoon the cheese into lightly oiled ramekins or moulds. Once the cheese is cool, cover it with cling film and keep it in the refrigerator.

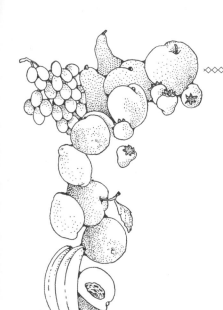

PART 4

MARMALADE

Marmalade has become a traditional
spread for buttered toast eaten at the
breakfast table. It is usually made with
citrus fruits and can range from thick and
dark with large pieces of peel, to light
and translucent with hardly any trace
of peel at all.

MAKING MARMALADE

Although modern marmalade is largely associated with oranges,
the original preserve was made from quince –
marmelo in Portuguese.

Today, the vast majority of marmalades are based on one of the members of the citrus family, even if other fruits are added to adjust the balance of acidity. The secret to good marmalade is the citrus peel, which adds a certain amount of bitterness to counteract the sweetness. In some recipes the peel is left in quite large pieces while in others it is shredded, so the type of marmalade you choose to make will depend on your family's taste. For those who don't like any peel at all, there are recipes for marmalade jelly which will give you all the flavour without any peel suspended in the preserve.

The favoured fruit for making marmalade is the Seville orange, which has an intensely sharp, almost bitter tang. This sharpness balances with the sweetness of the sugar beautifully, resulting in a flavour that is hard to beat.

You won't need to buy any extra equipment for making marmalade, but you will require patience as marmalade cannot be rushed. It will take longer to cook than a jam or jelly, as citrus peel needs lengthy, slow cooking to render it soft and palatable.

There's absolutely nothing to beat the flavour of homemade marmalade, and once you have made your first batch you will never want to return to buying the often over-sweet variety found on the supermarket shelves. Try a mixture of fruits and experiment with your own flavours and textures.

TIPS FOR MAKING MARMALADE

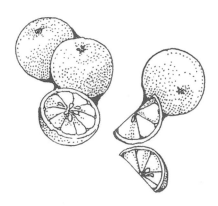

- Try to buy unwaxed fruit if possible. If you can't obtain it, always scrub the peel well before using.

- Use a vegetable peeler to remove a thin layer of peel from citrus fruits, as the white pith can impart a bitter flavour to the marmalade.

- Roll the fruit under the palm of your hand before using it. This helps to break down the tiny cells holding the juice.

- If the recipe calls for coarse-cut peel, soak it in water for a few hours before cooking to help reduce the cooking time.

- Reserve any pips, tie them in a muslin bag and add to the pan as they will help the marmalade to set. Remove the bag before potting.

- Shredded peel tends to swell slightly during cooking, so always cut it slightly thinner than required.

- Soak whole fruit in a bowl of boiling water for a couple of minutes as this will help to loosen the peel and make it easier to remove. Use the soaking water in place of some of the water in the recipe as some of the citrus flavour will have leached into the water.

- Make sure you check that the peel is tender before adding sugar, because it will not get any softer once the mixture has been sweetened.

- Test for set as you would for jam (see page 24 for different methods of doing this).

APRICOT & ORANGE MARMALADE

The combination of apricot and orange gives this marmalade
a smoother texture. Try it on warm croissants for breakfast.

INGREDIENTS *Makes 1.5kg/3lb 3oz*
2 Seville oranges, washed and
    quartered (including peel)
1 lemon, washed and quartered
1.2 litres/2 pints water
900g/2lb apricots, stoned and
    thinly sliced
900g/2lb granulated sugar,
    warmed

METHOD
1. Prepare the oranges and
lemon and place the pips in a
muslin bag tied with string. Use
a food processor to chop the
oranges and lemon into small
pieces and then place
in a preserving pan with
the muslin bag and water.
2. Bring the mixture to the boil,
then reduce the heat until it is
just simmering. Cover the pan
and cook for 1 hour.
3. Add the sliced apricots and

bring the mixture back to the boil.
Turn down the heat once again
and allow the mixture to simmer
for a further 40 minutes, or until
the fruit is really soft.
4. Reduce the heat and add the
sugar. Cook over a low heat until
the sugar is dissolved, stirring
from time to time. Increase the
heat and bring the marmalade
back to the boil. Boil rapidly for
15 minutes, stirring occasionally,
or until setting point is reached.
5. Remove the pan from the
heat, skim off any scum with
a slotted spoon and leave to
cool for 5 minutes.
6. Stir to make sure the fruit is
evenly distributed, then
pour into hot,
sterilized jars
and seal.
Label
when cold.

GRAPEFRUIT MARMALADE

For a wonderful red blush and a delightfully tangy marmalade, choose a variety of grapefruit with red flesh.

INGREDIENTS *Makes 1.8kg/4lb*
900g/2lb grapefruit, preferably
    ruby red variety
1 lemon
1.2 litres/2 pints water
1.35kg/3lb granulated sugar,
    warmed

METHOD
1. Wash the grapefruit and dry on a clean tea towel. Remove the peel using a vegetable peeler and slice it into thin strips.
2. Cut the grapefruit and lemon in half and extract the juice using a lemon squeezer. Tie the pips inside a piece of muslin and attach to the side of a preserving pan with string, making sure the string is long enough for the muslin bag to hang in the liquid.
3. Put the fruit juice and strips of peel into the preserving pan with the water and bring to the boil. Reduce the heat, cover, and simmer for 2 hours or until the peel is very tender. Remove the muslin bag and leave it to cool. Once it is cool enough to handle, squeeze any juice back into the pan with your hands.
4. Add the sugar and stir over a low heat until it has completely dissolved. Increase the heat and boil the marmalade rapidly for 10–15 minutes or until it has reached setting point. Test every 5 minutes after 10 minutes of boiling, as the time it takes to set will vary from batch to batch.
5. Remove the pan from the heat, skim off any scum and leave the marmalade to cool for about 10 minutes. Stir to make sure the peel is evenly distributed, then pour into hot, sterilized jars. Seal and label when cold.

LEMON & LIME MARMALADE

In this delicious recipe, make sure you slice the lime peel very thinly as it tends to take longer to cook than that of other citrus fruits.

INGREDIENTS *Makes 1.5kg/3lb 3oz*
225g/8oz lemons
225g/8oz limes
1.4 litres/2½ pints water
1.1kg/2½lb granulated sugar,
    warmed

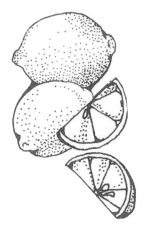

METHOD
1. Wash the lemons and limes, dry them thoroughly on a clean tea towel, then cut in half and extract the juice using a lemon squeezer. Put the juice in a jug, cover with cling film and place in the refrigerator for use the next day.
2. Scoop out the pulp and pips from the fruit and tie them in a muslin bag. Tie a piece of string around the top of the muslin bag and hang it from the side of your preserving pan.
3. Slice the peel from the lemons and limes into matchsticks and place them in the pan with the water and muslin bag. Cover with cling film and leave to soak overnight.
4. The following day, place the preserving pan over a low heat, cover, and let the marmalade simmer until the peel is really soft. Make sure you keep the pan covered during cooking to avoid losing too much liquid through evaporation. The peel should be sufficiently soft to break apart

easily when squeezed between your finger and thumb.

5. Remove the muslin bag containing the pips. When it's cool enough to handle, squeeze it over the pan to extract the last bit of juice and the pectin in the pips and then discard.

6. Add the sugar and the reserved lemon and lime juice to the pan and, over a low heat, stir until the sugar has dissolved completely. The easiest way to check this is to inspect the back of the wooden spoon make sure there are no signs of sugar crystals.

7. Turn up the heat and bring the liquid to a rolling boil until setting point has been reached. Start checking after 10 minutes of cooking and then at regular 5-minute intervals until you are satisfied that it has reached the correct consistency.

8. Remove the pan from the heat and leave the marmalade to cool for about 10 minutes. Give it one final stir before potting to make sure that the peel is evenly distributed.

9. Use a ladle or jam funnel to transfer the marmalade into hot, sterilized jars. Seal them immediately and, when cool, wipe down the outside of the jars with a warm, damp cloth. Label before storing.

VARIATION

For a Christmassy variation, add 225g/8oz of fresh cranberries at the end of step 5 and simmer for 15–20 minutes or until the berries have popped and softened. This will need to be done before you add the sugar. Try this marmalade as an accompaniment to cold turkey – it works surprisingly well. If fresh cranberries aren't available, frozen ones work equally well.

LEMON & GINGER MARMALADE

In this unusual variation on conventional marmalade, lemon and ginger make a winning combination. This recipe makes a great present, as it's unlikely to be found in the shops.

INGREDIENTS *Makes 1.8kg/4lb*
1.1kg/2½lb lemons
140g/5oz fresh root ginger, peeled
1.2 litres/2 pints water
900g/2lb granulated sugar,
    warmed

METHOD
1. Wash the lemons and dry them on a clean tea towel. Quarter and slice the fruit, reserving the pips. Tie the pips in a piece of muslin and secure it to the side of the preserving pan with a piece of string.
2. Grate the ginger, discarding any tough, hairy parts as these will remain tough even when cooked.
3. Put the lemon, ginger and water into the pan, bring to the boil, then turn down the heat. Cover the pan and simmer gently for 2 hours or until the fruit is really tender.
4. Remove the muslin bag, leave it to cool and then squeeze over the pan to release all the juice and pectin.
5. Add the sugar and continue cooking over a low heat, stirring until the sugar has dissolved completely. Increase the heat and boil for a further 5–10 minutes or until setting point has been reached.
6. Remove the pan from the heat and, with a slotted spoon, skim off any scum from the surface of the marmalade. Leave to cool for 5 minutes, then give it a final stir to ensure the fruit is well distributed.
7. Pour the marmalade into hot, sterilized jars and seal. When cool, label and store.

ORANGE & WHISKY MARMALADE

Adding a little whisky to marmalade after it has reached setting point gives it a wonderful depth of flavour and turns an ordinary orange preserve into something really special.

INGREDIENTS *Makes 1.1kg/2¹/₂lb*
450g/1lb Seville oranges
1.7 litres/3 pints water
1.35kg/3lb granulated sugar, warmed
4 tbsp lemon juice
90ml (3fl oz) whisky

METHOD

1. Scrub the oranges and cut them in half. Using a lemon squeezer, press the juice from the oranges into a large bowl and place it in the refrigerator.

2. Place the pips and most of the pith in a piece of muslin secured with string to make a little bag.

3. Cut the orange peel into thin shreds and place in a bowl. Cover with the water and add the muslin bag. Leave the peel to soak overnight.

4. The following day, tip the water, peel and muslin bag into a preserving pan, tying the bag to the side. Simmer for about 2 hours or until the peel is tender. Remove the muslin bag, leave it to cool and then squeeze the juices back into the pan.

5. Add the sugar and orange and lemon juice and stir over a low heat until the sugar has dissolved completely. Increase the heat and boil rapidly for 15 minutes, or until setting point is reached.

6. Remove the pan from the heat, skim off any scum and stir the whisky into the hot marmalade. Leave it to cool slightly in the pan and as it starts to thicken give it a good stir to make sure all the peel is evenly distributed.

7. Ladle into hot, sterilized jars and seal immediately. Label and store once cool.

OXFORD MARMALADE

There is a world of difference between home produced Oxford marmalade and the commercial version. Made properly, it should be very dark and sweet, yet retain a touch of bitterness.

INGREDIENTS *Makes 2.25kg/5lb*
900g/2lb Seville oranges
1.7 litres/3 pints water
1.35kg/3lb granulated sugar,
   warmed

METHOD

1. Scrub the oranges, then pare using a vegetable peeler. Cut the peel into thick, chunky slices and put them in a preserving pan.

2. Cut the oranges into small pieces, reserving the pips. Add the orange pieces to the preserving pan and tie the pips into a square of muslin secured with a piece of string. Add the muslin bag and water to the pan.

3. Bring the mixture to the boil, then turn down the heat, cover the pan and simmer for 2 hours or until the fruit and peel are soft. Top up with water to the original level if the marmalade appears to be too dry.

4. Remove the pan from the heat and leave the mixture to infuse overnight.

5. The following day, remove the muslin bag, squeeze to release the juices and return the pan to the heat. Bring to the boil, cover and simmer for 1 hour.

6. Add the sugar to the pan, then slowly bring the mixture to the boil, stirring until the sugar has dissolved. Turn up the heat and boil rapidly for 15 minutes or until setting point is reached.

7. Take the pan off the heat and skim off any scum that has formed on the surface. Leave the mixture to cool for 5 minutes, then stir again to distribute the peel.

8. Ladle into hot, sterilized jars and seal. Label when cool.

PEACH & ORANGE MARMALADE

This recipe for a soft-set preserve makes a nice change from the thicker marmalades. It is delicious on hot buttered crumpets.

INGREDIENTS *Makes 1.8kg/4lb*
2 Seville oranges
2.25kg/5lb fresh peaches,
    prepared weight
1.35kg/3lb granulated sugar,
    warmed

METHOD

1. Scrub the oranges and grate the peel coarsely, taking care not to grate too deeply into the surface, as you do not want to grate the pith. Peel off all the pith and break the oranges into segments. Place the membranes and pips in a muslin square tied securely with a piece of string.

2. Place the peaches in boiling water for 1 minute, then rinse them under the cold tap. Once they are cool enough to handle, peel off the outer skin and chop the flesh into small pieces, discarding the stones.

3. Put the grated peel, orange segments, muslin bag and peach flesh into a preserving pan and bring to the boil. Reduce the heat, cover, and simmer until the peach pieces are soft – about 30 minutes.

4. Remove the muslin bag and allow to cool. Squeeze the juices back into the pan, then add the sugar. Cook over a low heat, stirring, until the sugar has dissolved. Increase the heat and bring the marmalade to a rapid boil for 15 minutes or until setting point is reached. Stir occasionally during this time, squashing the peach chunks on the side of the pan so they combine thoroughly.

5. Remove from the heat, skim off any scum and leave to stand for about 5 minutes. Give the marmalade one final stir then ladle into hot, sterilized jars and seal. Label when cool.

PINEAPPLE MARMALADE

In this lively twist on a traditional breakfast marmalade, succulent pineapple is complemented by the sharp, refreshing flavour of grapefruit.

INGREDIENTS *Makes 2.25kg/5lb*
3 grapefruit
900ml/1½ pints water
2 × 425g/14oz cans crushed
    pineapple in its own juice
900g/2lb granulated sugar,
    warmed

METHOD

1. Wash the grapefruit, cut them in half and squeeze out the juice using a lemon squeezer. Reserve the membranes, pith and pips and tie into a square of muslin secured with a piece of string. Slice the grapefruit peel finely (3mm/¹⁄₈in) and put into a preserving pan with the juice, water and muslin bag and bring to the boil.

2. Reduce the heat, cover the pan and simmer gently for 1½–2 hours, or until the peel is tender, stirring the mixture from time to time.

3. Add the pineapple and its juice and simmer for a further 30 minutes.

4. Remove the muslin bag, allow it to cool and then squeeze the juices back into the pan. Add the sugar and heat gently, stirring, until it has dissolved completely. Turn up the heat and boil rapidly for 10 minutes, or until setting point is reached.

5. Take the pan off the heat, skim off any scum using a slotted spoon and leave the marmalade to cool for about 10 minutes.

6. Give the mixture one final stir to make sure the peel is evenly distributed throughout the marmalade, then pour into hot, sterilized jars. Seal immediately and label when cool.

SPICY KUMQUAT MARMALADE

————•◦◦●◦◦•————

A delightful marmalade to brighten up any grey day, with the
lovely sweet-sour flavour of kumquat.

INGREDIENTS *Makes 2.25kg/5lb*
24 kumquats
2 Navel oranges
2.5cm/1in fresh root ginger,
    peeled and thinly sliced
2 cinnamon sticks
1 tsp freshly grated nutmeg
about 2 litres/3½ pints water
about 1.8kg/4lb granulated
    sugar, warmed
the juice of 2 lemons

METHOD
1. Wash the kumquats and
oranges, dry on a clean tea towel
then chop finely, reserving the
pips from the oranges. Put the
pips, ginger, cinnamon and
nutmeg inside a square of muslin
and secure with a piece of string.
2. Using a mug as a measure,
place 3 mugfuls of water for every
mugful of fruit into a large bowl.
Add the muslin bag and leave to

stand in a cool place overnight.
3. Next day, put the contents of the
bowl into a preserving pan, tying
the muslin bag to the side, and
bring to the boil. Reduce the heat
and simmer for 1½–2 hours or until
the peel of the fruit is very tender.
4. Remove from the heat, take out
the muslin bag and, when cool
enough to handle, squeeze the
juices back into the pan. Measure
the fruit and add 1 mug of sugar
for every mug of fruit. Mix in the
lemon juice.
5. Return the fruit to the pan and
bring to the boil. Reduce the
heat and stir until the sugar has
dissolved. Increase the heat and
boil rapidly for about 15 minutes
or until it reaches setting point.
6. Remove the pan from the heat
and skim off any scum. Put the
marmalade into hot, sterilized jars
and seal. Label when cool.

TANGERINE MARMALADE

Tangerines give this jelly marmalade a sweeter flavour than ones made from Seville oranges. It is a preserve that children will love.

INGREDIENTS *Makes 2.25kg/5lb*
900g/2lb tangerines
2 lemons
1 grapefruit
4 litres/7 pints water
450g/1lb sugar to every 600ml/
   1 pint of juice

METHOD

1. Wash the fruit and dry it on a clean tea towel. Cut the tangerines, lemons and grapefruit in half and squeeze out all the juices. Reserve the pips, membranes and pith.

2. Pare the peel and cut into fine strips, keeping the tangerine peel separate from that of the lemon and grapefruit.

3. Put the pips, membrane, pith and the lemon and grapefruit peel into a piece of muslin and tie it securely with a piece of string.

4. Put the tangerine peel in a large bowl with the muslin bag and the fruit juices. Add the water and leave to soak overnight.

5. The following day, tip the mixture into a preserving pan, bring to the boil, then turn down the heat and simmer gently it for 1½–2 hours. Remove the muslin bag.

6. Measure the juice and put the pan on a medium heat. Add the sugar in the quantity given in the ingredients and stir over a low heat until the sugar has dissolved.

7. Add the tangerine peel and bring to the boil. Boil rapidly for approximately 1 hour until the marmalade reaches setting point. Remove the scum and pot the marmalade in hot, sterilized jars. Seal immediately then label and store once the jars are cool.

THREE-FRUIT MARMALADE

This traditional marmalade uses three citrus fruits. It's your choice as to just how chunky you decide to make it!

INGREDIENTS *Makes 2.25kg/5lb*
2 grapefruit
3 Seville oranges
1 lemon
2.2 litres/4 pints water
1.5kg/3lb 3oz granulated sugar, warmed

METHOD

1. Scrub the fruit and dry it on a clean tea towel. Cut the grapefruit into quarters and the lemon and oranges in half and put them in a saucepan with a tight-fitting lid. Add the water and bring to the boil. Turn down the heat and simmer for about 1 hour or until the peel of the fruit is so soft you can easily push a knife into it.

2. Using a slotted spoon, remove the fruit from the pan, reserving the water it was cooked in. Leave the fruit to cool on a plate. When it is cool enough to handle, cut it into thin pieces, depending on how fine or coarse you would like your finished marmalade to be. Discard any pips.

3. Transfer the fruit and the water it was cooked in to a preserving pan. Add the sugar, then heat gently, stirring all the time until the sugar has dissolved completely.

4. Turn up the heat and bring the marmalade to a rolling boil. After about 15 minutes, start testing to see if it has reached setting point.

5. Remove the pan from the heat, skim off any scum and leave to cool for 5 minutes. Give it a final stir before placing in hot, sterilized jars. Seal immediately and label once the jars are cool.

TOMATO MARMALADE

Green tomatoes have many culinary uses, but perhaps one of the most unusual is this tangy preserve which can double up as a relish.

INGREDIENTS *Makes 2.25kg/5lb*
5 lemons
400ml/14fl oz water
900g/2lb green tomatoes
1.5kg/3lb 3oz granulated sugar,
   warmed

METHOD
1. Wash the lemons, halve them and squeeze out the juice using a lemon squeezer. Set aside. Place the remaining flesh, membranes and pips in a square of muslin.
2. Remove the pith from the inside of the peel with a sharp knife and cut the peel into fine strips. Put them in a pan, add the water and simmer, covered, for 20 minutes.
3. Wash and dry the tomatoes, then cut into quarters. Remove the core and seeds, put them into the muslin with the lemon and secure

it with a piece of string. Chop the tomato flesh into small pieces and put into a preserving pan with the lemon juice made up to 1.7 litres/3 pints with water. Add the softened lemon peel and liquid and the muslin bag, tied to the side of the pan, and bring to the boil. Reduce the heat and simmer for about 40 minutes or until the fruit is soft.
4. Remove the muslin bag and, when it is cool enough to handle, squeeze any liquid back into the pan. Add the sugar and heat gently, stirring, until it has completely dissolved. Turn up the heat and boil rapidly until setting point is reached, stirring from time to time.
5. Remove from the heat, skim any scum from the surface, then ladle the preserve into hot, sterilized jars.

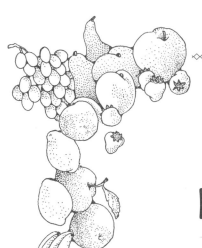

PART 5

CHUTNEYS

The process of making chutney is similar to that of jam, with the same reward of jars of delicious homemade goodies to eat. Chutneys are made from finely cut vegetables and fruit with different spices added to give a range of flavours. A good chutney depends upon the blending of the ingredients so that they balance and complement one another.

MAKING CHUTNEY

Chutney isn't hard to make, but consuming it requires patience!
It should never be eaten straight away, but left to mature for a few
months so that the spices can penetrate the other ingredients.

Chutney can be made from almost any fruit and vegetable combination. One important rule to remember is that you must never use equipment made of copper or brass, as the acid in the vinegar will react with the metal and spoil the finished preserve. Use only enamel, stainless steel or aluminium pans, and nylon sieves and wooden spoons.

TIPS FOR MAKING CHUTNEY

- Use good-quality vinegar as it has a more intense flavour.

- Using ground spices rather than whole will achieve a more piquant flavour. If you do want to use whole spices, bruise them and then tie them inside a muslin bag.

- If a recipe calls for ginger, you can either use the fresh root or dried ground ginger. One unit of ground ginger is equivalent to 1½ units of root ginger.

- Except for the vinegar and sugar, all the ingredients should be cooked for the same length of time. The addition of late-added ingredients means that the flavour of these will dominate and the texture of the chutney will be rougher.

- Chutney requires long, slow cooking. Evaporation is an important part of the process, so make sure you always cook chutney uncovered.

- The type of sugar you choose for your recipe will affect the

flavour and colour of the end result. Brown sugar gives the richest flavour and the darkest colour; demerara and golden granulated sugars give the chutney a caramel flavour; and white sugar produces light-coloured chutneys.

- As the chutney starts to thicken towards the end of the cooking time, you will need to stir it frequently to prevent it from sticking to the bottom of the pan and burning.

- If you find your chutney has become too thick, add a little more vinegar, remembering that chutneys thicken considerably as they cool.

- Chutney can keep for months, even years, if stored in the right conditions, so make sure it is kept in a cool, dark place.

THINGS THAT CAN GO WRONG

- If you find that your chutney starts to dry out and shrink away from the sides of the jar, it means that you did not have an airtight seal when putting on the lid after potting up.

- If a dark layer forms at the top of the jar or the whole contents of the jar start to darken, this usually indicates some form of contamination. Alternatively, it may be caused by not having an airtight seal; by using jars that have not been sterilized correctly; or by storing the chutney for too long at too warm a temperature.

APPLE & TOMATO CHUTNEY

This chutney is a good way to use up tomatoes at the height of the growing season. The blend of spices gives it a rich flavour that will do justice to any cold platter.

INGREDIENTS *Makes 2.25kg/5lb*
1kg/2¼lb cooking apples, peeled, cored and thinly sliced
1kg/2¼lb red tomatoes
450g/1lb onions, chopped
2 garlic cloves, finely chopped
1 tbsp mustard seeds
250g/9oz sultanas
1 tsp salt
3 tsp curry powder
1 tsp cayenne pepper
1.2 litres/2 pints malt vinegar
450g/1lb demerara sugar

METHOD

1. Put the apples in a saucepan with a little water. Heat to simmering point, cook until tender, then drain.

2. Place the tomatoes in boiling water for 2 minutes. When cool enough to handle, peel off the skins and discard them along with the cores and seeds. Slice the flesh roughly and put into a preserving pan with the drained apple. Add the onion and garlic to the pan.

3. Put the mustard seeds inside a square of muslin and tie with string to make a little bag.

4. Add the mustard bag to the pan, together with the sultanas, salt, curry powder, cayenne pepper and half the quantity of malt vinegar. Bring to the boil and simmer until the ingredients are soft.

5. Add the sugar and the remaining vinegar and cook slowly, stirring constantly, until the sugar has dissolved. Continue to cook until the chutney is smooth and thick. Remove the muslin bag and immediately transfer the chutney to jars.

APPLE, DATE & CHILLI CHUTNEY

You can reduce the amount of chillies in this recipe to suit your taste. The sweetness of the dates also helps to tame the heat and produces a spicy chutney that goes well with cheese or cold meats.

INGREDIENTS *Makes 2.25kg/5lb*

1.8kg/4lb cooking apples, peeled, cored and chopped into small pieces

2 onions, chopped

300ml/10fl oz water

3 cloves garlic, finely chopped

250g/9oz dates, stoned and chopped

2 red chillies, deseeded and finely chopped

600ml/1 pint distilled white malt vinegar

750g/1lb 10oz dark muscovado sugar

1 tsp salt

40g/1¼oz ground ginger

1 tbsp ground cinnamon

½ tsp ground cumin

METHOD

1. Put the apples and onions in a preserving pan with the water and bring to the boil. Reduce the heat and simmer for 20 minutes or until soft.

2. Drain off the water, then add the remaining ingredients. Cook over a low heat, stirring constantly, until the sugar has dissolved, and then increase the heat to medium and cook, uncovered, for about 90 minutes, stirring from time to time to stop the chutney from sticking.

3. When the mixture is thick enough to leave a trail when you run a wooden spoon across it, remove from the heat and ladle into hot, sterilized jars. Place a waxed disc on the surface and seal immediately.

4. Once the chutney is cool, wipe the jars with a warm, damp cloth and label them. Keep for at least two months before using.

APRICOT CHUTNEY

The spices are quite subtle in this recipe to allow the true taste of the apricots to come through. It's great with strong cheeses or with curries as an alternative to mango chutney.

INGREDIENTS *Makes 1kg/2¹/4lb*
250g/9oz dried apricots
1 onion, finely chopped
115g/4oz seedless golden raisins
115g/4oz sultanas
3 garlic cloves, crushed
the juice and grated zest of 1
    lemon
1 tsp grated fresh root ginger
1 tsp salt
1tsp coriander seeds
600ml/1 pint white malt vinegar
450g/1lb golden granulated
    sugar
450g/1lb apples, peeled, cored
    and grated

METHOD
1. Cut the apricots into small pieces and soak them in water for 3 hours to soften them.

2. Drain the apricots and place them in a preserving pan with the onion, raisins, sultanas, crushed garlic, juice and zest of the lemon, grated ginger, salt, coriander seeds and half the quantity of malt vinegar.
3. Bring the mixture to the boil, turn down the heat, then simmer for 30 minutes.
4. Add the sugar, the grated apples and the remaining vinegar and cook gently, stirring, until the sugar has dissolved. Cook slowly until the mixture thickens, stirring occasionally to prevent it from sticking to the bottom of the pan.
5. Remove the pan from the heat, leave the contents to settle for 5 minutes, then ladle into hot, sterilized jars and seal immediately.

BEETROOT CHUTNEY

Beetroot absorbs the flavours of the vinegar and spices to produce
a deep-red spicy chutney that can be eaten in sandwiches or used
to accompany a summer salad.

INGREDIENTS *Makes 1.8kg/4lb*
1kg/1¼lb raw beetroot, peeled
    and grated
450g/1lb onions, finely chopped
750g/1lb 10oz cooking apples,
    peeled, cored and finely
    chopped
the zest and juice of 3 oranges
2 garlic cloves, finely chopped
450g/1lb seedless raisins
1 tbsp ground ginger
1 tbsp coriander seeds
1kg/1¼lb golden granulated
    sugar
1 litre/1¾ pints red malt vinegar

METHOD
1. Prepare the fruit and
vegetables and place them in
a preserving pan, along with all
the remaining ingredients. Bring
the mixture to a gentle simmer
and stir until the sugar has

dissolved. Cook for 1 hour, stirring
frequently, until the chutney is
thick and the fruit and vegetables
are tender.

2. Once the chutney is ready,
leave it to settle for 10 minutes and
then spoon into hot,
sterilized jars
and seal
immediately.
You can eat it straight
away, but the flavour
will improve if you
keep it for a month.

- - - - - - - - - - - - - - - -
TOP TIP

To avoid staining your
hands, wear rubber gloves
when preparing the beetroot.
- - - - - - - - - - - - - - - -

BLACKBERRY & APPLE CHUTNEY

Blackberries give chutneys a wonderful flavour but need to be rubbed through a sieve to remove the pips. This fruity chutney enhances any red meat or duck roast.

INGREDIENTS *Makes 4kg/8¹/₂lb*
2.7kg/6lb blackberries
1kg/2¼lb cooking apples, peeled, cored and finely chopped
1kg/2¼lb onions, finely chopped
30g/1oz salt
60g/2oz mustard powder
60g/2oz ground ginger
2 tsp ground mace
1 tsp cayenne pepper
1 litre/1¾ pints malt vinegar
1kg/2¼lb brown sugar

METHOD
1. Wash and drain the blackberries, remove any stalks then simmer in a little water for 20 minutes. When cooked, rub the blackberries through a fine nylon sieve. Discard the pips.
2. Prepare the apples and onions and place in a preserving pan with the blackberry pulp and all

the remaining ingredients except the sugar.
3. Bring to the boil, reduce the heat and simmer for 1 hour or until the fruit is soft and pulpy.
4. Add the sugar and cook, stirring, until it has completely dissolved. Continue to cook over a medium heat until the chutney becomes thick.
5. Ladle into jars while still hot and seal immediately.

VARIATION

If you like your chutney to have a kick, add 2 large red chillies, finely chopped, with the other ingredients.

GREEN TOMATO CHUTNEY

This is another really good recipe for using up tomatoes left on the vine at the end of the season.

INGREDIENTS *Makes 2.5kg/5¹/₂lb*
1.8kg/4lb green tomatoes,
   roughly chopped
450g/1lb cooking apples, peeled,
   cored and roughly chopped
450g/1lb onions, finely chopped
2 large garlic cloves, finely
   chopped
1 tbsp salt
3 tbsp pickling spice
600ml/1 pint cider vinegar
450g/1lb white granulated sugar

METHOD
1. Prepare the tomatoes, apples, onions and garlic and put in a preserving pan with the salt.
2. Put the pickling spice inside a square of muslin and tie securely with a piece of string. Place the bag inside the pan.
3. Add half the quantity of vinegar and bring to the boil. Reduce the heat and simmer gently for 1 hour or until the chutney has reduced in volume and is starting to thicken. Make sure you stir at regular intervals to stop it from sticking.
4. Add the sugar and the remaining vinegar and heat gently, stirring, until the sugar has dissolved. Simmer gently for 1½ hours or until the chutney is thick, stirring from time to time.
5. Take the pan off the heat, remove the muslin bag and pot the chutney immediately in hot, sterilized jars.

GREENGAGE CHUTNEY

Greengage chutney is exceptionally easy to make and goes really well with grilled mackerel or any other oily fish.

INGREDIENTS *Makes 2.7kg/6lb*

1.8kg/4lb greengages, quartered
and stones removed
3 cooking apples, peeled, cored
and chopped
3 onions, chopped
450g/1lb golden seedless raisins
6 garlic cloves, crushed
6 red chillies, chopped (including
the seeds)
2 tbsp pickling spice,
in a muslin bag
1 tsp sea salt
1.5 litres/2¾ pints white
wine vinegar
1.1kg/2½lb golden granulated
sugar

METHOD

1. Put all the ingredients into a preserving pan. Bring to the boil, reduce the heat and stir until the sugar has dissolved completely.
2. Continue to cook gently for 2 hours or until all the liquid has evaporated and the chutney has thickened. Remember to stir it occasionally to prevent it from sticking to the bottom of the pan.
3. Take the chutney off the heat, remove the muslin bag and immediately ladle it into hot, sterilized jars.

PICKLING SPICE

This combination of spices, available in most supermarkets, usually contains cinnamon, mustard seed, bay leaves, allspice, dill seeds, cloves, ginger, peppercorns, coriander, juniper berries, mace and cardamom.

MANGO CHUTNEY

This chutney is regularly served at Indian restaurants to be eaten as a relish with poppadoms or to accompany the main dish.

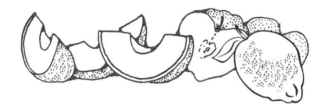

INGREDIENTS *Makes 1kg/2¹/4lb*
900g/2lb ripe mangoes, peeled, stoned and cut into cubes
½ tsp salt
300ml/10fl oz white wine vinegar
200g/7oz demerara sugar
225g/8oz cooking apples, peeled, cored and roughly chopped
1 onion, finely chopped
1 garlic clove, crushed
5cm/2in fresh root ginger, grated

METHOD

1. Prepare the mangoes and place them in a non-metallic bowl. Sprinkle with the salt and set aside.

2. Put the vinegar and sugar into a preserving pan and heat gently, stirring constantly, until the sugar has dissolved completely.

3. Add the mango, apple, onion and garlic to the pan and bring the mixture to a boil, stirring occasionally. Reduce the heat until the mixture is simmering and cook for 1 hour or until the liquid has evaporated and the chutney has thickened.

4. Spoon the chutney into hot, sterilized jars and seal immediately. Leave it to mature for 2–3 weeks before serving.

PEAR & WALNUT CHUTNEY

Pear and walnut chutney has a mellow flavour that complements the pungency of stronger cheeses such as stilton or gorgonzola. It's fine to use windfall pears provided that you cut out any bruised or damaged parts of the fruit.

INGREDIENTS *Makes 1.8kg/4lb*
1.1kg/2½lb pears, peeled, cored and roughly chopped
2 medium-sized cooking apples, peeled, cored and roughly chopped
225g/8oz onions, finely chopped
900ml/1½ pints cider vinegar
225g/8oz sultanas
the grated zest and juice of 1 orange
450g/1lb soft brown sugar
115g/4oz walnuts, chopped
2 tsp ground cinnamon

METHOD
1. Wash and prepare the pears, apples and onions. Put them into a preserving pan with the vinegar and stir well.
2. Bring the mixture to a boil then reduce the heat to a simmer. Cook for around 40 minutes, stirring occasionally.
3. While the mixture is cooking, soak the sultanas in the orange juice in a small bowl.
4. Add the sugar, sultanas and orange zest and juice to the preserving pan. Heat gently, stirring until the sugar has dissolved. Continue to simmer for a further 40 minutes or until the liquid has evaporated and the chutney has thickened.
5. Toast the walnuts in a dry, non-stick frying pan for about 5 minutes over a low heat until they are lightly coloured. Add them to the preserving pan with the ground cinnamon and stir to combine.
6. Ladle the chutney into hot, sterilized jars and seal.

PLUM CHUTNEY

This is a spicy version of plum chutney; you will find that the chilli bursts on your tongue a few seconds after the sweet fruit flavour.

INGREDIENTS *Makes 1.1kg/2¹/2lb*
1.35kg/3lb plums
500ml/16fl oz white wine vinegar
4 garlic cloves, finely sliced
175g/6oz dried apricots, chopped
600g/1lb 5oz white granulated
   sugar
1 whole lemon, finely chopped
   with pips removed
1 tsp cayenne pepper
1 tsp ground coriander
4 red chillies, finely sliced
   (including the seeds)
1 tsp salt
1 tsp allspice
1 tsp cinnamon
1 tsp ground ginger
5 juniper berries
10 black peppercorns

METHOD
1. Put the whole plums in a saucepan with the vinegar, bring to the boil and then take off the heat. Leave to soak overnight.

2. The following day, remove the stones from the softened fruit and put the plums and vinegar into a preserving pan. Add the rest of the ingredients, with the exception of the sugar.

3. Bring the mixture to simmering point then add the sugar. Stir constantly until you are certain the sugar has dissolved.

4. Turn up the heat to medium and cook the chutney for 1½–2 hours, stirring occasionally to stop it from burning. Once the liquid has evaporated and the chutney has thickened, it is ready to pour into hot, sterilized jars.

This chutney improves with keeping. You can give it even more kick by adding some dried chilli flakes during the thickening process.

PUMPKIN CHUTNEY

This is a chutney that can be enjoyed at Halloween, using up the leftover flesh once you have made a pumpkin lantern. Try it with some full-bodied Cheddar cheese.

INGREDIENTS *Makes 1.8kg/4lb*
1.35kg/3lb pumpkin flesh
4 ripe tomatoes
2 cooking apples
250g/9oz onions
60g/2oz sultanas
750g/1lb 10oz soft brown sugar
2 garlic cloves, crushed
2 tsp ground ginger
2 tsp allspice
2 tsp freshly ground black pepper
1 tsp salt
600ml/1 pint malt vinegar
1 tbsp fresh tarragon, finely
   chopped

METHOD
1. Prepare the pumpkin by removing the rind and seeds and chopping the flesh into cubes about 1cm/½in in diameter.
2. Skin the tomatoes by steeping them in boiling water for 2 minutes, then roughly chop. Peel the apples, remove and discard the cores and roughly chop the flesh. Chop the onions.
3. With the exception of the fresh tarragon, place all the ingredients into a preserving pan and bring the mixture to a boil. Reduce the heat to a simmer and cook gently for 30–45 minutes or until the pumpkin is tender. Continue to cook until the liquid has evaporated and the chutney has thickened.
4. Remove the pan from the heat, add the chopped tarragon and stir to combine. Spoon the chutney into hot, sterilized jars, cover with wax discs and seal with airtight lids. Keep for 2–3 weeks before eating.

RED GRAPE CHUTNEY

Try serving this chutney instead of apple sauce when you next have
a slow-roasted belly of pork.

INGREDIENTS *Makes 1.1kg/2¹/2lb*
900g/2lb red grapes
900g/2lb cooking apples, peeled,
    cored and finely chopped
450g/1lb white granulated sugar
450ml/15fl oz red wine vinegar
the finely grated zest and
    juice of 1 lime
½ tsp salt
1 tsp ground cinnamon
1 tsp freshly grated nutmeg

METHOD
1. If the grapes are large, cut
them in half and remove any
seeds. Small seedless ones may
be left whole.
2. Prepare the apples and put
them in a preserving pan with
the grapes, sugar and vinegar.
Bring the mixture slowly to the
boil and stir until the sugar has
dissolved completely.
3. Reduce the heat and simmer

the chutney for about 45 minutes
or until the fruit is tender.
4. Stir in the grated lime zest
and juice, together with the salt,
cinnamon and nutmeg. Continue
to simmer the chutney for about
15 minutes or until the liquid has
evaporated and the chutney
has thickened.
5. Spoon the hot chutney into
prepared jars, cover with a
waxed disc and seal.

RED ONION CHUTNEY

In this recipe the onions are caramelized first to make the finished chutney dark and sticky, with a wonderful flavour.

INGREDIENTS *Makes 1.35kg/3lb*

1.35kg/3lb red onions, peeled and chopped into short, thin slices

1 red chilli, chopped into short, thin slices (including the seeds)

2 bay leaves

3 tbsp olive oil

200g/7oz brown sugar

3 tbsp balsamic vinegar

90ml/3fl oz brown malt vinegar

2 garlic cloves, crushed

1 tsp ground cinnamon

1 tsp freshly grated nutmeg

1 tsp ground ginger

2 tsp ground coriander

2 tsp salt

1 tsp freshly ground black pepper

METHOD

1. Place the onions and chilli in a frying pan with the bay leaves and olive oil and cook gently over a medium heat for about 20 minutes, or until the onions are dark and sticky.

2. Put the caramelized onions into a preserving pan and add the sugar, vinegars, garlic cloves, spices and salt and pepper. Heat gently, stirring continuously until the sugar has dissolved completely.

3. Continue to simmer the mixture for about 2–3 hours, or until the liquid has reduced and the chutney has thickened, stirring occasionally to prevent it sticking to the bottom of the pan.

4. Remove from the heat, ladle into hot, sterilized jars and seal immediately. Label with the contents and date once the chutney has cooled down. It will improve with keeping, so leave it for about a month before opening. This chutney is delicious with soft cheese.

RHUBARB & GINGER CHUTNEY

The rhubarb it is added late in this recipe to retain its shape and colour. This chutney is delicious with roast gammon.

INGREDIENTS *Makes 1.35kg/3lb*
1 large onion, finely chopped
300ml/10fl oz distilled malt
    vinegar
4 whole cloves
1 cinnamon stick
the zest of 1 orange, grated
400g/14oz white granulated
    sugar
150g/5½oz sultanas
1kg/2¼lb rhubarb, cut into
    2.5cm/1in pieces
5cm/2in fresh root ginger,
    grated

METHOD

1. Place the onion in a preserving pan with the vinegar, cloves and cinnamon stick. Bring the mixture to a boil, then reduce the heat and simmer gently for 10 minutes, or until the onion is tender.
2. Add the grated orange zest to the pan along with the sugar and sultanas. Simmer gently, stirring constantly, until the sugar has dissolved. Continue to cook at this heat for a further 10–15 minutes or until the liquid has formed a thick syrup.
3. Add the rhubarb and grated ginger to the pan and cook gently for a further 15 minutes, or until the rhubarb is soft. Gently stir the chutney from time to time, being careful not to break up the rhubarb pieces too much.
At the end of the cooking time there will still be a little liquid left, but the chutney should have thickened nicely.
4. Leave to stand for 5 minutes, then stir again so that the rhubarb is evenly distributed. Ladle into hot, sterilized jars, cover with waxed circles and seal immediately. Label once the chutney has cooled.

SPICY INDIAN CHUTNEY

Chutneys are an integral part of Indian cuisine, complementing a broad range of spicy dishes.

INGREDIENTS *Makes 2.25kg/5lb*
1kg/2¼lb cooking apples, peeled,
   cored and roughly chopped
450g/1lb onions, finely chopped
8 garlic cloves, crushed
1.2 litres/2 pints malt vinegar
60g/2oz salt
450g/1lb seedless raisins
115g/4oz mustard powder
140g/5oz ground ginger
4 tsp cayenne pepper
900g/2lb soft brown sugar

METHOD

1. Place the apples, onions and crushed garlic cloves in a preserving pan together with the vinegar. Bring to the boil then reduce the heat to a simmer and cook for about 20–25 minutes or until the apples and onions are soft.

2. Remove the pan from the heat and stir in the salt, raisins, mustard powder, ginger and cayenne pepper. Cover the pan with a clean tea towel and leave it overnight for the flavours to infuse.

3. The following day, add the brown sugar to the preserving pan and return to the heat. Bring slowly to simmering point, stirring constantly until all the sugar has dissolved.

4. Continue to cook for a further 40–50 minutes or until the liquid has evaporated and you are left with a thick chutney.

5. Remove the pan from the heat and leave to stand for 5 minutes. Give it one final stir before putting into hot, sterilized jars. Add a waxed disc to the top of each jar and seal with airtight lids. This chutney improves with age, so wait a month before eating.

SWEET PEPPER CHUTNEY

This chutney combines the natural sweetness of red, green and orange peppers with spices to create a condiment full of flavour.

INGREDIENTS *Makes 1.35kg/3lb*
450g/1lb ripe tomatoes
1 red pepper, deseeded and
    finely chopped
1 green pepper, deseeded and
    finely chopped
1 orange pepper, deseeded and
    finely chopped
350g/12oz onions, finely chopped
450g/1lb cooking apples, peeled,
    cored and roughly chopped
500ml/16fl oz malt vinegar
1 tsp mustard seeds
2 tsp black peppercorns
250g/9oz demerara sugar
1 tsp ground allspice

METHOD
1. Skin the tomatoes by blanching in boiling water for 2 minutes and then roughly chop the flesh. Prepare the peppers, onions and cooking apples and place them in a preserving pan together with the tomatoes and vinegar.

2. Put the mustard seeds and peppercorns inside a square of muslin, secure with a piece of string and add to the pan.

3. Bring the mixture to the boil, then reduce the heat and simmer for about 20 minutes or until the fruit and vegetables are soft.

4. Add the sugar and allspice and stir until the sugar has dissolved. Continue to simmer until the liquid has evaporated and the chutney has thickened.

5. Take the pan off the heat, remove the muslin bag containing the spices and leave to stand for 5 minutes. Stir briefly before ladling into hot, sterilized jars. Add a label once the jars are cool.

TOMATO & MUSTARD SEED CHUTNEY

Tomato chutney is a great way of using up tomatoes, particularly when they all seem to ripen in the same week!

INGREDIENTS *Makes 1.1kg/2½lb*
1kg/2¼lb ripe tomatoes
450g/1lb onions, finely chopped
2 garlic cloves, finely chopped
2 sweet eating apples, peeled,
    cored and roughly chopped
2 tsp mustard seeds
200g/7oz soft brown sugar
600ml/1 pint malt vinegar

METHOD
1. Skin the tomatoes by steeping them in boiling water for 2 minutes. Once they are cool enough to handle, slip off the skins. Roughly chop the flesh and put into a preserving pan with the onions, garlic, apples, mustard seeds, sugar and about three-quarters of the vinegar.
2. Bring the mixture to the boil, stirring continuously until the sugar has dissolved. Reduce the heat and simmer for about 40 minutes, stirring occasionally. At the end of the cooking time the mixture should have the consistency of a wet paste.
3. Add the remaining vinegar to the chutney, stir and continue to cook for a further 30–40 minutes or until the liquid has evaporated and the chutney has thickened. If the consistency is still too liquid after this time, continue cooking the chutney for a further 10–15 minutes.
4. Remove the pan from the heat and ladle the mixture into hot, sterilized jars. Place a disc of waxed paper directly on top and seal with airtight lids while still hot. This chutney is best if it is allowed to mature for at least one month before eating.

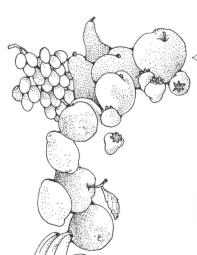

PART 6

PICKLES

Unlike chutneys, pickles are quick and easy to prepare. They are made by preserving raw or lightly cooked vegetables in a spicy vinegar. It is easy to create a vast range of pickles that will last for months and it's a great way of preserving fruit and vegetables so that they are available all year round.

MAKING PICKLES

Almost any fruit or vegetable can be preserved by the action of acetic acid in vinegar. By preparing the vinegars with a range of spices in advance you give the flavours time to infuse, resulting in a far superior pickle.

Pickles are made in three stages. First you make the vinegar; then you add raw or partially cooked fruits and vegetables to it; finally you pot and seal the finished pickle. You don't need special equipment to make pickles, but it's advisable to have a deep glass bowl for layering the vegetables during the salting process (this is a necessary stage in some of the recipes on the following pages).

Kilner jars with their rubber seals are ideal for pickles, as are large glass jars with plastic lids such as old coffee jars. Never use a jar with a metal lid as the acid will eventually attack the metal and cause it to corrode.

When it comes to bottling, the jar should be full but not packed too tightly, as there needs to be space for the vinegar to surround each piece of fruit and vegetable. The jar should be filled right to the top. Take care to ensure there are no trapped air bubbles otherwise the contents may quickly discolour.

All fruits and vegetables used for pickling should be picked when they are at their prime, preferably while still young. Smaller fruits and vegetables can be pickled whole, while larger vegetables, such as cauliflower, red cabbage and cucumbers, will obviously need to be chopped or sliced first.

If you are making clear pickles, the vegetables will initally need to be soaked in brine; the salt helps to draw out the moisture and makes it easier for the vegetables to absorb the vinegar. Use only pure sea salt or kosher salt, as regular table or cooking salt contains iodine and other additives which can taint the pickle and make it cloudy.

If you are making sweet pickles you will need to cook the fruits or vegetables before bottling. They are then preserved in a sweet vinegar.

If you want a soft pickle – for example, one made with apricots or marrow – the method is slightly different. Here the fruit is packed into hot jars, then boiling hot pickling vinegar is poured over it and the jars are sealed while still hot.

Most of the cooked pickles can be used after a week; they also store well. Uncooked pickles should be left to mature for about two months before eating.

PREPARING THE VINEGAR

- Always use the best possible quality vinegar when making pickles; the cheaper ones will give the pickle an acid tang

rather than a subtle flavour. The most suitable types are malt vinegars or distilled brown or white vinegars.

- Use whole spices rather than ground and give the vinegar time to mature. To enhance the flavour of the spices, you can dry-fry them first.

- Adjust the amount of spices in the vinegar according to whether you want a mild or hot spicy pickle.

- Tie the spices in a muslin bag before putting them in the vinegar rather than dropping them straight into the liquid.

- Use a jar with a tight lid and shake it occasionally.

- If you have fruit or vegetables with a thick skin, such as lemons, and you require a softer texture, they will need to be cooked in brine before pickling in vinegar.

FOR A MILD PICKLE

1.2 litres/2 pints malt or distilled
vinegar (brown or white)
10g/¼oz of each of the following:
cinnamon stick, whole cloves,
whole mace, allspice and
white peppercorns

FOR A HOT PICKLE

1.2 litres/2 pints malt or distilled
vinegar (brown or white)
10g/¼oz of each of the following:
cinnamon stick, whole cloves,
whole mace, allspice and
white peppercorns
5cm/2in fresh root ginger, peeled
and sliced
30g/1oz mustard seed
15g/½oz black peppercorns
15g/½oz crushed chillies,
including seeds

FOR A SWEET PICKLE

1.2 litres/2 pints malt or distilled
vinegar (brown or white)
250g/9oz soft brown sugar
10g/¼oz salt
5cm/2in fresh root ginger, peeled
and sliced
½ tsp whole mixed spice

½ tsp white peppercorns
4 whole cloves

All the above vinegars should
be left for at least a month for the
flavours to infuse; remember
to shake them once a week.
Any of the recipes in this section
of the book can be made with
these pickling vinegars, or you
can use the ones specified for
each individual pickle.

THE QUICK METHOD

If you have some fruit or
vegetables that you want to
pickle and you don't have any
vinegar made in advance, you
can cheat and use the quick
method. Put the vinegar and
spices (not in a muslin bag this
time) into a bowl, cover with a
lid or kitchen foil and place the
bowl in a saucepan of cold water.
Bring the water to the boil then
remove the pan from the heat
and leave the bowl in the water
to cool for a couple of hours.
Strain the vinegar through a fine
sieve before using.

FRUIT-INFUSED VINEGARS

Sweet pickles can be improved by using vinegars infused with fruit, such as raspberry, or lemon or orange zest. You can buy these ready prepared, but as they are very simple to make you might like to have a go at preparing them yourself. The following recipes make 750ml/1¼ pints and should be used within a year.

RASPBERRY VINEGAR

450g/1lb fresh raspberries
600ml/1 pint white wine vinegar

METHOD

1. Wash the raspberries, drain well, then put them in a bowl and cover with the vinegar. Drape a clean tea towel over the bowl and leave it in a cool place for 5 days, stirring once each day. Strain the vinegar through a nylon sieve and discard the raspberries. Pour the vinegar into a jelly bag suspended over a bowl and leave to drain until it has stopped dripping. Store in sterilized bottles.

LEMON AND THYME VINEGAR

Follow the instructions as for raspberry vinegar (above), but use 2–3 sprigs of fresh thyme and the thinly pared zest of 1 lemon instead of the raspberries. Wash and drain the thyme and bruise slightly by hitting it gently with a rolling pin. Add the thyme and lemon to the vinegar and follow the recipe as before.

PICKLED APPLE

Pickled apples are delicious served with boiled gammon, pork chops or cold meats.

INGREDIENTS *Makes 1.35kg/3lb*
750ml/1¼ pints raspberry vinegar
(see page 117)
1 cinnamon stick
5cm/2in fresh root ginger, peeled
and sliced
6 whole cloves
1.35kg/3lb eating apples, peeled,
cored and halved
750g/1lb 10oz granulated sugar

METHOD
1. Put the vinegar in a stainless steel saucepan and add the cinnamon stick, ginger and cloves. Bring the vinegar to the boil then reduce the heat and simmer gently for about 5 minutes.
2. Gently drop the apple halves into the vinegar with a spoon, then continue to simmer for 5–10 minutes until they are just tender but not too soft – the fruit should still be quite firm when it is bottled.
3. Use a slotted spoon to remove the apples from the pan and pack them into hot, sterilized jars.
4. Add the sugar to the vinegar and stir over a gentle heat until completely dissolved.
5. Once the sugar has dissolved, increase the heat and boil rapidly for 5 minutes, or until the liquid has reduced and started to thicken slightly.
6. Strain the syrup through a fine sieve then pour it over the apples in the jars so that they are completely immersed. Seal immediately and label when cold.

PICKLED BEETROOT

This is one of the most popular vegetables for pickling, not only for its colour but also for the sweet flavour that permeates the vinegar.

INGREDIENTS *Makes 1.5kg/3lb 3oz*
2kg/4½lb fresh beetroot
1–1.5 litres/1¾–2¾ pints malt
   vinegar
1 tbsp coriander seeds
4 whole cloves
1 tbsp black peppercorns
1 bay leaf
1 cinnamon stick
85g/3oz soft brown sugar

METHOD
1. Preheat the oven to 180°C/
350°F/gas mark 4.
2. Cut the stalks from the beetroot, leaving about 2.5cm/1in intact. Wash the beetroot but don't damage the skin by scrubbing too hard. Dry on kitchen paper then wrap in kitchen foil. Bake in the oven for 2 hours. Check whether the beetroot are cooked by piercing them with a knife; if it goes in easily, they are done.

3. Put the vinegar, coriander, cloves, peppercorns, bay leaf and cinnamon into a stainless steel saucepan and warm gently. Add the sugar and stir until it has completely dissolved. Turn up the heat and boil for about a minute, then turn off the heat and cover the pan.
4. Leave the flavours to infuse for 2 hours, then drain the vinegar through a fine nylon sieve.
5. Remove the skin from the beetroot and cut the flesh into 5mm/¼in slices. Place the sliced beetroot in sterilized jars and pour in the pickling vinegar, making sure the beetroot are immersed and the jars are full to the brim.
6. Seal and store in a cool, dark place for a few weeks before eating. Try this pickle with salads or on open sandwiches.

CAULIFLOWER & BROCCOLI PICKLE

Pickling cauliflower and broccoli ensures that the family can enjoy these vegetables all year round.

INGREDIENTS *Makes 1.5kg/3lb 3oz*

1 head of cauliflower, fresh and
   tightly packed
2 heads of fresh broccoli
salt water (see recipe)
1 litre/1¾ pints white
   wine vinegar
5 blades of mace
1 tsp coriander seeds
1 tsp mustard seeds
1 cinnamon stick
6 black peppercorns
4 small red chillies, pierced and
   left whole
3 bay leaves

METHOD

1. Cut away the leaves from the cauliflower and break the heads into small florets with your fingers rather than cutting them apart.
2. Cut away the large woody stem from the broccoli and then break the heads into small florets.

3. Weigh the florets; for every 450g/1lb you will need to dissolve 60g/2oz salt in 600ml/1 pint water. Wash the florets, shake dry and then soak overnight in the water.
4. Put the vinegar and the spices, chillies and bay leaves into a stainless steel saucepan and bring to the boil. Remove from the heat, cover and leave overnight for the flavours to infuse.
5. The next day, drain the florets and rinse under cold running water to remove the salt. Leave to dry in a colander, then pack tightly in sterilized jars. Leave 2.5cm/1in of space at the top so that the florets can be completely covered by the vinegar.
6. Pour the cold vinegar, including the spices, over the broccoli and cauliflower and seal the jars immediately. Store for two months before eating.

CLASSIC PLOUGHMAN'S PICKLE

It is hard to beat a delicious ploughman's lunch with crusty bread and your favourite cheese, but it is the pickle that makes it great.

INGREDIENTS *Makes 1.5kg/3lb 3oz*

250g/9oz carrots
140g/5oz dried apricots
140g/5oz prunes, stoned
2 courgettes, chopped
1 medium cauliflower, broken
    into small florets
10 garlic cloves, crushed
140g/5oz raisins
2 onions, chopped
2 cooking apples, peeled, cored
    and chopped
225g/8oz muscovado sugar
1 tsp sea salt
60ml/2fl oz lemon juice
350ml/11fl oz cider vinegar
200ml/7fl oz malt vinegar
1 tbsp Worcestershire sauce
2 tsp black mustard seeds
1 tsp ground allspice
1 tsp ground black pepper

METHOD

1. Chop the carrots, apricots, prunes, apples and courgettes into small cubes. Try to make them as even in size as possible.

2. Put all the ingredients into a large preserving pan and bring to the boil. Reduce the heat to a simmer and cook for 1½–2 hours, or until the vegetables are *al dente*. Take care not to overcook them because they should retain some of their crunch.

3. If the mixture is still quite runny at the end of the cooking time, take a ladleful of the vinegar from the pan and mix it with 1 tablespoon of cornflour or arrowroot to make a paste. Return it to the pan and cook for 5 minutes, stirring until the mixture has thickened.

4. Allow to cool before bottling in sterilized jars.

CRUNCHY COURGETTE PICKLE

This is delicious served with Cheddar cheese and crusty bread
or spooned over hamburgers as a relish.

INGREDIENTS *Makes 500g/1lb 2oz*
500g/1lb 2oz courgettes,
   finely sliced
3 shallots, finely chopped
2 tbsp sea salt

FOR THE PICKLING VINEGAR:
500ml/16fl oz cider vinegar
140g/5oz golden caster sugar
1 tsp dry mustard powder
1 tsp mustard seeds
1 tsp celery seeds
1 tsp ground turmeric
½ dried chilli, crushed

METHOD

1. Place the courgette
slices in a glass bowl
with the chopped
shallots and sprinkle
them with the salt.
Cover with ice-cold
water and stir until the
salt has completely

dissolved. Leave the vegetables to
soak for 1 hour then drain and dry
them with kitchen paper or clean
tea towels.

2. Place all the ingredients for the
pickling vinegar in a stainless
steel saucepan and bring gently
to a simmer, stirring until the
sugar has dissolved completely.
Remove the pan from the heat
and leave it until it is warm to
the touch.

3. Add the courgette slices and
shallots to the pan and stir until
they are thoroughly coated
in the vinegar.

4. Spoon the contents of the
saucepan into sterilized jars,
seal immediately and leave
for a week before eating.
This pickle should be kept in
the refrigerator and eaten
within two months.

CUCUMBER WITH DILL PICKLE

Even though they are steeped in liquid, these cucumbers remain crunchy, and they are deliciously flavoured with dill.

INGREDIENTS *Makes 900g/2lb*
3 large cucumbers, thinly sliced
50g/1¾oz sea salt
600ml/1 pint cider vinegar
450g/1lb soft brown sugar
1 tbsp whole mustard seeds
1 tbsp dill seeds
1 large handful of fresh dill,
 roughly chopped
2 large onions, finely chopped

METHOD
1. Layer the cucumber slices with the salt in a large plastic or glass dish. Put a plate on top of the cucumber, weight it down with some large tins and leave for at least 4 hours so that the salt draws out the water from the cucumber.
2. Tip the cucumber out into a large colander and rinse thoroughly under cold water to get rid of all the salt.
3. Gently heat the vinegar in a stainless steel saucepan, add the sugar and stir until it is dissolved.
4. Add the mustard and dill seeds and fresh dill. Next add the cucumber and onion and bring to the boil. Cook for a minute then drain, reserving the liquid.
5. Return the liquid to the saucepan and boil rapidly until it has reduced by one-third.
6. Put the cucumber and onion into hot jars then pour the vinegar syrup over the top and seal the jars immediately. The vegetables must be completely immersed in the liquid.

There is no need to leave this pickle to mature. Once it has been opened, keep it in the refrigerator. If you decide to use small cucumbers instead of large ones, simply slice them lenthways into four strips.

MIXED VEGETABLE PICKLE

This simple pickle is often used as an accompaniment to Asian dishes or eaten with homemade flat breads. You will need to spend a little time preparing the vegetables, but the pickle is easy to make and can be eaten straight away .

INGREDIENTS *Makes 450g/1lb*

½ cauliflower head, broken into
    tiny florets
2 carrots, sliced
2 celery sticks, thinly sliced
¼ white or red cabbage, thinly
    sliced
115g/4oz runner beans, cut into
    bite-sized pieces
4 garlic cloves, finely sliced
2 fresh red chillies, deseeded and
    finely sliced
5cm/2in fresh root ginger, peeled
    and finely sliced
1 red pepper, thinly sliced
2 tsp salt
½ tsp turmeric
5 tsp mustard seeds
1 tsp fenugreek seeds
1 tbsp golden granulated sugar
4–6 tbsp olive oil
the juice of 1 lemon

METHOD

1. Prepare all the vegetables, put them in a large bowl and sprinkle with the salt. Leave them to stand for about 4 hours so that the salt draws liquid from the vegetables.

2. Drain the vegetables in a colander and shake to remove any excess liquid.

3. Transfer the vegetables to a clean bowl and mix in all the remaining ingredients. Stir to combine thoroughly then cover the bowl and chill for at least an hour before you are ready to serve it.

MUSHROOM & GARLIC PICKLE

You can use any mushrooms you like for this pickle – it works best if you use a wide assortment.

INGREDIENTS *Makes 900g/2lb*
500g/1lb 2oz mixed mushrooms
    such as chestnut, shiitake,
    giroles, oyster and small
    button mushrooms
300ml/10 fl oz cider vinegar
1 tbsp sea salt
1 tsp caster sugar
300ml/10 fl oz water
4 sprigs of fresh thyme
4 garlic cloves, slivered
1 small red onion, sliced
3 small dried red chillies
1 tsp coriander seeds, crushed
10 whole black peppercorns
360ml/12fl oz extra virgin olive oil,
    or sufficient to cover

METHOD
1. Trim all the mushroom stalks and cut the larger mushrooms in half.
2. Combine the vinegar, salt, sugar and water in a large stainless steel saucepan. Bring it to the boil then add the thyme, garlic, onion, chillies, coriander and peppercorns and simmer for 2 minutes.
3. Add the mushrooms to the pan and turn down the heat to a simmer. Cook for 3–4 minutes and then drain through a fine sieve, retaining any herbs and spices. Leave to drain until the sieve stops dripping.
4. Put the mushrooms into hot, sterilized jars and distribute the onion, garlic, herbs and spices evenly between the jars.
5. Pour the olive oil into the jars and make sure the ingredients are fully covered. Tap the jars to dispel any air bubbles, then seal and store them in the refrigerator. This pickle does not have a very long shelf life and needs to be eaten within two weeks.

PICCALILLI

Piccalilli, or mustard pickle, is the colour of sunshine and brightens up any cheese board. It is delicious with pork pies.

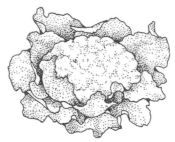

INGREDIENTS *Makes 1.35kg/3lb*
140g/5oz sea salt
1.5 litres/2¾ pints cold water
300g/10oz cauliflower florets
175g/6oz gherkins
115g/4oz celeriac
115g/4oz green pepper
4 pickling onions, quartered

FOR THE PICKLING VINEGAR:
600ml/1 pint malt vinegar
2 tsp mixed pickling spice

FOR THE SAUCE:
30g/1oz plain flour
1 tbsp mustard powder
½ tbsp turmeric
½ tsp ground mace

2 tsp ground ginger
3 tbsp malt vinegar
strained spice vinegar

METHOD
1. Mix the salt and water together in a bowl large enough to take all the vegetables.
2. Cut the cauliflower, gherkins, celeriac and pepper into 5mm/¼in dice, making sure that the pieces are approximately the same size.
3. Place the vegetables, including the pickling onions, into the salted water and leave to soak for 24 hours. To make sure they stay immersed, place a weighted plate on top.

To make the pickling vinegar:
Put the vinegar and all the spices into a stainless steel saucepan and bring to simmering point over a medium heat. Lower the heat, cover the pan and simmer gently for 15 minutes. Leave to cool.

To make the sauce:
1. Blend the flour, mustard powder, turmeric, mace and ginger in a bowl, add the malt vinegar and stir until you have a smooth paste. Gradually strain the pickling vinegar over the paste, stirring as you go to make sure the mixture is smooth and free of lumps.
2. Pour the sauce into a large saucepan and stir it over a low heat until it starts to thicken. It should be thick enough to coat the back of a wooden spoon.

To complete the piccalilli:
1. Drain the vegetables from the brine and shake well to get rid of any excess moisture. There is no need to rinse off the salt because

there is no extra salt added to the sauce mixture.
2. Add the vegetables to the sauce and bring to simmering point over a medium heat. Cook for only 1 minute after it reaches this point as the vegetables should retain their natural crunch.
3. Stir the pickle gently to make sure that all the vegetables are coated in the sauce. Ladle into hot, sterilized jars and seal immediately. Label when cool and store for a month to allow the piccalilli to mature before eating.

VARIATION

If you don't like the taste of green pepper, you can replace it with cucumber, carrot, beans, marrow, courgette or any other vegetables you have to hand.

PICKLED CHERRY TOMATOES

These are delicious as an appetizer or part of a mixed buffet – in fact
their sweet flavour goes with almost anything.

INGREDIENTS *Makes 1.8kg/4lb*
1.8kg/4lb firm cherry tomatoes
1.5kg/3lb 3oz white sugar
1 litre/1¾ pints water
6cm/2½in fresh root ginger,
    grated
the grated zest and juice of 2
    lemons
1 red chilli, deseeded and
    finely chopped
1 tsp salt

METHOD
1. Wash the cherry tomatoes and
prick each one with a fork.
2. Put the sugar and water in a
large saucepan and place over
a medium heat, stirring until the
sugar has completely dissolved.
Turn up the heat and boil rapidly
for 5 minutes.
3. Add the cherry tomatoes and
cook for 10 minutes. With a slotted
spoon, remove the tomatoes from
the pan and set aside.
4. Add the grated ginger, lemon
zest and juice, chilli and salt to
the pan. Bring the mixture back
to the boil, then reduce the heat
to a simmer. Cook for 15 minutes.
5. Put the tomatoes back into the
pan with the cooking liquid and
simmer for a further 30 minutes
or until the liquid has started
to evaporate and has formed a
thick syrup.
6. Pour the tomato mixture into
hot, sterilized jars and seal
immediately.

PICKLED EGGS

Pickled eggs were introduced in the days before refrigeration. Today, they are wonderful for picnics or camping when you want a snack that doesn't require any cooking.

INGREDIENTS *Makes 12 eggs*
12 large, very fresh eggs
360ml/12fl oz distilled white
    vinegar
360ml/12fl oz water
1 tbsp pickling spice
1 garlic clove, crushed
1 bay leaf
6 black peppercorns

METHOD
1. Put the eggs in a large saucepan and cover them completely with cold water. Bring to the boil, then immediately remove the pan from the heat. Cover the pan and leave the eggs to stand in the hot water for 12 minutes.
2. Remove the eggs from the hot water, place in cold water for 2 minutes, then remove the shells.
3. In a medium saucepan, mix together the vinegar, water and pickling spice. Bring to the boil then add the garlic, bay leaf and peppercorns. Remove from the heat.
4. Transfer the eggs to hot, sterilized jars and add the hot vinegar mixture, making sure that the eggs are fully immersed. Seal and keep in a cool place for 8–10 days before serving.

VARIATION

To add a bit of colour to your eggs, replace the water with liquid from your pickled beetroot (page 119).

PICKLED ONIONS

The humble onion is the perfect vegetable for pickling, as it retains its crispness and its natural sweet flavour.

INGREDIENTS *Makes 1kg/2¹/₂lb*

1kg/2¼lb small pickling onions
  or shallots
115g/4oz sea salt
750ml/1¼ pints malt vinegar
1 tbsp sugar
2–3 dried chillies
1 tsp mustard seeds
1 tbsp coriander seeds
1 tsp allspice
1 tsp black peppercorns
5cm/2in fresh root ginger, sliced
3 blades of mace
4 fresh bay leaves

METHOD

1. Make sure that the onions are firm, with unbroken skins; shallots should not have any growth shoots as this usually means they are past their best. Trim the tops and bottoms off the onions and drop them into a bowl of boiling water. Leave to stand for about 4–5 minutes; you should then be able to peel off the skin with ease.

2. Put the onions in a bowl and cover with cold water to measure the quantity required. Drain this water into a saucepan, add the salt and heat slightly until the salt has dissolved. Leave to cool before pouring back over the onions in the bowl. To keep the onions submerged, put a weighted plate on top. Leave them to stand for 24 hours.

3. Put the malt vinegar and sugar into a large stainless steel saucepan.

4. Place all the remaining ingredients, except the bay leaves, into a square of muslin and secure tightly with a piece of string. Drop the muslin bag into the saucepan.

5. Bring the vinegar to the boil, stirring to dissolve the sugar, then turn down the heat and simmer for 5 minutes. Remove the pan from the heat, cover with a clean tea towel and leave to infuse for 24 hours.

6. The following day, drain the onions and leave them to dry on several layers of kitchen paper.

7. Pack the onions into sterilized jars then open the muslin bag

and distribute the spices evenly between the jars.

8. Pour the vinegar over the onions, making sure they are completely immersed, then add a bay leaf to each of the jars.

9. Seal the jars and store them in a cool, dark place for at least 4–6 weeks before eating. The flavour of the onions will improve with keeping.

TOP TIPS

• If you have any vinegar left over from making the pickled onions, don't throw it away. Store it in a sterilized bottle for your second batch or use it in another pickle recipe.

• You can also pickle garlic cloves in this way – they are much milder than you might expect. Store for 8 weeks before eating.

PICKLED PLUMS

Any plums are suitable for this recipe as long as they are firm because the flesh softens very quickly. A pickle is a great way to preserve this juicy fruit; it goes well with a spicy curry.

INGREDIENTS *Makes 900g/2lb*
900g/2lb firm plums
150ml/5fl oz clear apple juice
450ml/15fl oz cider vinegar
½ tsp salt
8 juniper berries
2.5cm/1in fresh root ginger, peeled and cut into matchsticks
4 cloves
4 blades of mace
4 × 2.5cm/1in cinnamon sticks
2 dried chillies (optional)
675g/1½lb preserving sugar

METHOD
1. Wash and dry the plums, then prick them several times with a cocktail stick.
2. Put the apple juice, vinegar, salt, juniper berries, ginger, cloves, mace and cinnamon sticks into a preserving pan and bring slowly to the boil. If you like a spicy pickle, add the chillies to the other ingredients.
3. Add the plums to the pan and slowly bring it back to the boil. Reduce the heat and simmer gently for 10 minutes, or until the plums are just starting to soften. Remove the plums with a slotted spoon and pack them into hot, sterilized jars.
4. Add the sugar to the preserving pan and stir over a low heat until it has completely dissolved. Bring to a rolling boil and cook until the liquid has turned to a syrup.
5. Leave the syrup to cool slightly, then pour it over the plums in the jars. Seal immediately and store for at least a month before eating. Plums will keep for up to a year when preserved in this way.

PICKLED RED CABBAGE

The vibrant colour and flavour of pickled cabbage is good with many dishes, from a snack of bread and cheese to a dinner party of duck confit or roast goose.

INGREDIENTS *Makes 1kg/2¹/₄lb*
675g/1½lb red cabbage, finely
   shredded
1 large red onion, finely sliced
2 tbsp sea salt
600ml/1 pint red wine vinegar
the grated zest of 1 orange
85g/3oz golden caster sugar
1 tbsp coriander seeds, toasted
3 whole cloves
2.5cm/1in fresh root ginger
1 star anise
2 bay leaves
4 sweet eating apples, peeled,
   cored and grated

METHOD

1. Prepare the cabbage and the onion and place in a large glass bowl. Sprinkle with sea salt and mix well with your hands until the vegetables are coated in the salt. Turn the mixture into a colander sitting on top of a bowl and leave the vegetables to drain overnight.

2. The following day, rinse the cabbage and onion under cold running water and pat dry with kitchen paper.

3. Pour the vinegar into a stainless steel saucepan, add the orange zest, sugar, all of the spices and the bay leaves and bring to the boil. Remove the pan from the heat and set aside to cool.

4. Mix the apples with the cabbage and onions and then put into sterilized jars. Strain the spiced vinegar over the top, seal the jars and store for 7 days before eating. Alternatively, if you like your cabbage spicy, leave the spices in the vinegar rather than straining it when bottling up.

PICKLED WALNUTS

Pickled walnuts are an old English tradition usually eaten at Christmas with strong cheese or cold meats. As malt vinegar is a little harsh and can mask the delicate flavour of the walnuts, a gentler pickling vinegar is used instead.

INGREDIENTS *Makes 50 walnuts*

1.5 litres/2¾ pints cider vinegar

2 tbsp mixed white, pink and
   black peppercorns

9 cloves

2 tsp ground mace

5cm/2in fresh root ginger, peeled
   and grated

2 garlic cloves, finely chopped

175g/6oz dark molasses sugar

enough brine to cover the
   walnuts, using 45g/1½oz salt
   for every 250ml/9fl oz water

50 green walnuts

METHOD

1. Make your pickling spice at least 1–2 months in advance by putting all the ingredients into a stainless steel saucepan and bringing them to the boil. Turn down the heat immediately and simmer for about an hour. Allow to cool, then pour into sterilized bottles.

2. To make the brine, put the salt and water into a pan and boil until the salt has dissolved. Allow to cool.

3. Green (immature) walnuts are usually picked in June and July before the hard shell has had time to form. When you are handling walnuts it is advisable to wear rubber gloves as the clear juice they produce is a natural dye and can stain your hands dark brown. Pierce each walnut several times with a fork and then put them all in a large bowl. Cover them with the brine, making sure they are all immersed by placing a plate on top, and leave to soak for a week.

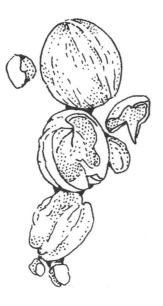

and store them in the refrigerator. Wait for a few weeks before eating the walnuts.

4. Drain the walnuts, make a new batch of brine, and soak them for a second week.

5. At the end of the soaking time, drain the walnuts and lay them out on trays to dry out for 2–4 days; as they dry, they will turn black. As soon as all the walnuts have changed colour, they are ready to pickle.

6. Spoon the walnuts into sterilized jars and fill them with the pickling vinegar to within 1cm/½in of the top. Seal the jars

- - - - - - - - - - - - - - - -

VARIATION

This recipe for a quick pickling vinegar means you don't have to make it in advance:

900ml/1½ pints malt vinegar
450g/1lb dark brown sugar
1 tsp ground allspice
½ tsp ground cinnamon
1 tbsp grated fresh
   root ginger

Put all the ingredients into a stainless steel saucepan and bring to the boil. Simmer over a medium heat for 15 minutes. Remove from the heat and allow the vinegar to cool before adding to the walnuts.

- - - - - - - - - - - - - - - -

PRESERVED LEMONS

Many Moroccan tagine recipes call for preserved lemons to give them a zesty flavour. This recipe is very easy and the preserved lemons taste far fresher than any shop-bought alternatives.

INGREDIENTS *Makes 12 lemons*

12 unwaxed lemons

12 tbsp coarse sea salt

2 tsp coriander seeds

4 dried chillies

1 cinnamon stick

300ml/10fl oz freshly squeezed
   lemon juice

METHOD

1. Scrub the peel of the lemons using a vegetable brush then dry them with kitchen paper. Cut off the little rounded bit at the stems, turn each lemon over and make a large cut by slicing lengthways, stopping about 2.5cm/1in from the bottom. Make a second cut so that you have marked the lemon with an 'X' shape.

2. Open up the lemons slightly and pack the middle of each one with a tablespoon of salt.

3. Put the lemons in large, wide-necked, sterilized Kilner jars. Add a few coriander seeds, 1 dried chilli and a piece of cinnamon stick to each jar.

4. Press the lemons firmly in the jar to release some of their juices, add the lemon juice, put on the lids and leave to stand overnight.

5. The following day, press the lemons down again. Repeat for 2–3 days until the lemons are completely covered with liquid. If necessary, add a little extra lemon juice.

6. After about a month the lemon peel should have softened and the lemons will be ready to eat. To use, rinse the preserved lemons well to remove the salt, then slice before adding them to your recipe.

SPICY ORANGES

These spicy oranges are great to serve up at Christmas time with a plate of pâté or cooked ham.

INGREDIENTS *Makes 1.1kg/2¹/₂lb*
6 oranges
750ml/1¼ pints white wine
  vinegar
900g/2lb granulated sugar
1 cinnamon stick
1 tsp whole allspice
8 whole cloves
2.5cm/1in fresh root ginger,
  peeled and sliced

METHOD
1. Scrub the oranges and cut them into round slices about 5mm/¼in thick, discarding any pips.
2. Put the orange slices into a preserving pan and cover with cold water. Bring the mixture to the boil, then reduce the heat and simmer gently for 5 minutes, or until the oranges slices are soft. Remove them with a slotted spoon and place in a large bowl. Discard the cooking liquid.

3. Put the vinegar and sugar into the preserving pan. Tie the cinnamon, allspice, cloves and ginger into a piece of muslin, securing it with a piece of string. Add the spice bag to the pan and slowly bring the mixture to the boil, stirring until the sugar has completely dissolved. Simmer for 1 minute.
4. Return the oranges to the pan and cook gently for 30 minutes or until they have a glazed appearance.
5. Remove the pan from the heat and, using a slotted spoon, transfer the orange slices into hot, sterilized jars.
6. Boil the liquid for 10 minutes or until it is syrupy. Allow to cool for a few minutes and then pour over the oranges, tapping the jars to expel air bubbles. Seal the jars immediately.

WATERMELON PICKLE

Watermelon rind is usually discarded when the flesh is eaten. This refreshing pickle is a great way to use the rind, as it retains its aromatic melon flavour.

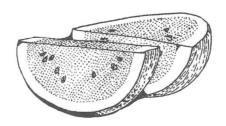

INGREDIENTS *Makes 900g/2lb*
900g/2lb watermelon rind
60g/2oz salt
900ml/1½ pints water
300ml/10fl oz white wine vinegar
450g/1lb preserving sugar
1 tsp whole cloves
1 tsp whole allspice
1 cinnamon stick
2.5cm/1in fresh root ginger,
    peeled and grated

METHOD

1. Using a sharp knife, remove the outer green rind of the watermelon, taking just a thin layer (about 3mm/⅛in) of the pink flesh.

2. Cut the rind into slices of about 5cm × 5mm/2in × ¼in. Put it into a large glass bowl. Dissolve the salt in the water then pour it over the melon rind. Cover with a weighted plate to make sure all the pieces are fully immersed and leave to soak overnight.

3. Drain the rind, rinse off any salt, put the rind into a preserving pan and cover with fresh water. Bring to the boil, reduce the heat and simmer for 10–15 minutes or until the rind is tender. Drain until it has stopped dripping.

4. Put the vinegar and sugar into a pan. Put the cloves, allspice, cinnamon and ginger into a square of muslin and tie securely with a piece of string. Add the bag to the preserving pan.

5. Heat the mixture gently, stirring until the sugar has dissolved, then bring it to the boil. Turn down the heat and allow the mixture to simmer for 10 minutes. Turn off the heat, add the melon rind, cover the pan with a clean tea towel and leave to stand for about 2–3 hours.

6. After the standing time, bring the pan back to the boil, then reduce the heat and simmer gently for 20 minutes, or until the rind is translucent.

7. Remove the spice bag, ladle the melon rind and syrup into hot, sterilized jars and seal. Leave to mature for 4 weeks.

WATERMELON CHUTNEY

900g/2lb watermelon rind
360ml/12fl oz cider vinegar
360ml/12fl oz water
450g/1lb granulated sugar
2.5cm/1in fresh root ginger, peeled and grated
2 fresh red chillies, peeled and chopped, with seeds
2 garlic cloves, finely chopped
1 tsp salt
½ tsp black peppercorns

Prepare the melon rind as in the main recipe, then put all the ingredients into a pan and heat, stirring until the sugar is dissolved. Reduce the heat and simmer until the rind is translucent and the liquid is syrupy (about 45 minutes). Transfer to hot, sterilized jars, seal immediately and leave for three weeks until the flavours have mellowed.

WICKED CHRISTMAS PEARS

These beautiful, pink pickled pears are a treat to bring out at Christmas and they go well with any leftover meats or cheeses.

INGREDIENTS *Makes 1.35kg/3lb*
1 lemon
450g/1lb golden granulated
　sugar
500ml/16fl oz raspberry vinegar
　(see page 117)
1 cinnamon stick
6 whole cloves
6 juniper berries, squeezed
　between the fingers
5cm/2in fresh root ginger, peeled
　and cut into matchsticks
150ml/5fl oz water
900g/2lb firm pears

METHOD
1. Using a vegetable peeler, remove a few strips of zest from the lemon, then squeeze out the juice using a lemon squeezer. Put the zest and juice into a large stainless steel pan and add the sugar, vinegar, spices and water. Heat gently, stirring until the sugar has dissolved, then slowly bring the liquid to the boil.

2. Prepare the pears by peeling, cutting them in half and scooping out the cores with a teaspoon.

3. Add the pears to the pan and simmer gently for 20 minutes or until the fruit is tender but still whole, taking care not to break them up.

4. Remove the pears with a slotted spoon and pack them into hot, sterilized jars, distributing the spices and lemon zest between the jars.

5. Boil the syrup for a further five minutes or until it has reduced slightly. Use a slotted spoon to skim off any scum from the surface and then ladle the syrup into the jars, making sure the pears are completely immersed. Cover and seal. Keep for a month before using.

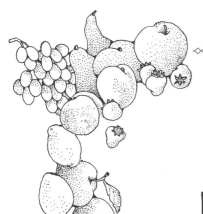

PART 7

RELISHES & KETCHUPS

While they are very similar to chutneys, relishes have a shorter shelf life and are quicker to prepare. Ketchups are a highly concentrated, seasoned blend of fruit and vegetable juices – a delicious accompaniment to many dishes.

MAKING RELISHES & KETCHUPS

You will find that the making of relishes and ketchups generally differs very little from any other preserving recipe you have tried, though individual methods may vary slightly.

The main difference between relishes and ketchups is their consistency. Ketchups are usually strained through a sieve to produce a smooth purée before bottling, while relishes are more chunky, with the fruit and vegetables cut into small pieces – halfway between a chutney and a pickle. They use the same fruits and vegetables as recipes earlier in this book, but tend to have bolder flavours. Not all the relishes require cooking, which makes them quick to prepare.

If stored properly, most ketchups and relishes will keep for several months without spoiling. They are so versatile that they can be used to accompany almost anything you fancy. There are no special pieces of equipment required other than those used for the earlier recipes. The rules about sterilizing apply as before.

TOP TIPS

To prevent fermentation and to give ketchups a longer shelf life, place the filled bottles or jars in a pan of water so that the water comes halfway up the jars. Cook over a gentle heat for 20–30 minutes, then allow to cool in the water.

CHILLI RELISH

This relish is great with any dish that needs a little spicing up.
It makes good use of an abundance of tomatoes and peppers, too.

INGREDIENTS *Makes 1.35kg/3lb*
800g/1¾lb ripe tomatoes, skinned
  and chopped
450g/1lb red onions, finely
  chopped
3 red peppers, deseeded and
  chopped
3 red chillies, deseeded and
  finely sliced
1 large cooking apple, peeled,
  cored and chopped
200g/7oz granulated sugar
200ml/7fl oz white wine vinegar
2 tsp celery seeds
2 tbsp mustard seeds
1 tbsp hot smoked paprika
1 tsp salt

METHOD
1. Put the prepared tomatoes,
onions, peppers, chillies and
apple into a preserving pan,
cover with a lid and cook over
a low heat for about 10 minutes,
or until the tomatoes start to
release their juices.
2. Add the sugar and vinegar
and bring slowly to the boil,
stirring continuously until the
sugar has dissolved. Add the
celery seeds, mustard seeds,
paprika and salt and stir to
combine all the ingredients.
3. Turn up the heat until the
mixture is at a slow boil and
cook, uncovered, for about 30
minutes. At the end of cooking
time, most of the liquid should
have evaporated and the mixture
will have a thick yet moist
consistency. Stir occasionally to
prevent it sticking to the bottom
of the pan.
4. Spoon the relish into hot,
sterilized jars, cover with
a waxed disc and seal
immediately. Leave to mature
for at least 2 weeks before using.

CORN RELISH

This bright yellow relish is crunchy and a great complement to any barbecued meat such as sausages, burgers or steaks.

INGREDIENTS *Makes 1kg/2¼lb*
6 fresh corn on the cob
280g/10oz white cabbage, finely
   shredded
2 small onions, finely sliced
500ml/16fl oz distilled malt
   vinegar
200g/7oz golden granulated
   sugar
1 red pepper, deseeded and
   finely chopped
1 tbsp plain flour
1 tsp mustard powder
½ tsp turmeric
1 tsp salt

METHOD

1. Put the corn cobs into a pan of boiling water and cook for 3 minutes. When they are cool enough to handle, strip the kernels from the cobs using a sharp knife.

2. Put the corn into a stainless steel saucepan with the cabbage and onion and all but 3 tablespoons of the vinegar. Add the sugar and slowly bring to the boil, stirring until the sugar has dissolved completely. Turn down the heat and simmer for 15 minutes. Add the red pepper and cook for a further 10 minutes.

3. Blend the flour, mustard, turmeric and salt with the reserved vinegar and mix until you have a smooth paste. Stir the paste into the vegetable mixture and bring back to the boil. Turn down the heat and simmer for a further 5 minutes or until the mixture has thickened.

4. Spoon the relish into hot, sterilized jars and seal.

CRANBERRY & PORT RELISH

This is a truly delicious alternative to cranberry sauce at Christmas time, enriched with a little port for sheer indulgence.

INGREDIENTS *Makes 900g/2lb*
450g/1lb red onions, finely sliced
2 tbsp olive oil
225g/8oz soft brown sugar
450g/1lb fresh cranberries
120ml/4fl oz red wine vinegar
120ml/4fl oz red wine
1 tbsp mustard seeds
2.5cm/2in fresh root ginger,
    peeled and grated
2 tbsp port
salt and freshly ground
    black pepper

METHOD
1. Prepare the onions and then heat the oil in a large saucepan. Add the onions and cook over a very low heat for about 15 minutes until soft.
2. Add 2 tablespoons of the sugar and cook for 5 minutes until the onions have caramelized.
3. Put the cranberries and remaining sugar in another saucepan together with the vinegar, wine, mustard seeds, and ginger. Stir over a low heat until the sugar has dissolved, then turn up the heat, cover and bring to the boil. Turn down the heat and simmer for 15 minutes or until the cranberries have burst.
4. Add the onions to the cranberry mixture and increase the heat slightly. Cook, uncovered, for 10 minutes, stirring frequently until the liquid has evaporated and the relish has thickened.
5. Remove from the heat, stir in the port and season with salt and pepper to taste. Spoon into hot, sterilized jars, cover with a waxed disc and seal immediately. Stored in a cool place. This relish keeps for up to 6 months.

CUCUMBER RELISH

A piquant relish that goes with almost anything. This is an excellent way to use up mis-shapen cucumbers.

INGREDIENTS *Makes 1.5kg/3lb 3oz*
900g/2lb cucumbers, diced
900g/2lb green tomatoes, diced
1 large onion, finely diced
1 green chilli, deseeded and
    finely sliced
2 tbsp salt
600ml/1 pint white wine vinegar
175g/6oz white sugar
½ tsp ground allspice
1 tbsp pickling spice
1 tsp mustard seeds

METHOD

1. Prepare the cucumbers, tomatoes, onion and chilli and layer them in a glass dish, sprinkling each layer with salt. Leave to stand overnight.
2. The following morning, tip the vegetables into a colander and drain well.
3. Put the vinegar, sugar and spices into a preserving pan and bring slowly to the boil, stirring continuously until the sugar has dissolved.
4. Once the sugar has dissolved, bring the liquid to the boil and add the vegetables. Reduce the heat to a simmer and cook, uncovered, for 30 minutes, stirring frequently, until the mixture is fairly thick but still moist.
5. Ladle the relish into hot, sterilized jars right up to the top, cover with a waxed disc and seal. Label the jars once they are cold. Leave for 4 weeks before eating. Once opened, store in the refrigerator.

NECTARINE & ORANGE RELISH

For those of you who like game for Christmas instead of the traditional turkey, try a spoonful of this relish as a condiment.

INGREDIENTS *Makes 450g/1lb*

3 tbsp olive oil

2 red onions, finely sliced

1 green chilli, deseeded and
    finely chopped

1 tsp finely chopped fresh
    rosemary

2 bay leaves

450g/1lb nectarines, stoned and
    cut into chunks

the grated zest and roughly
    chopped flesh of 1 orange

2 tsp coriander seeds

350g/12oz demerara sugar

200ml/7fl oz red wine vinegar

METHOD

1. Heat the oil in a large pan and add the onions, chilli, rosemary and bay leaves. Cook for 15 minutes or until the onions have softened.

2. Add the nectarines, orange zest and flesh, coriander seeds, sugar and vinegar and bring slowly to the boil. Stir until the sugar has dissolved completely.

3. Reduce the heat and simmer, uncovered, for 1 hour or until the liquid has evaporated and the relish is thick and sticky. Make sure you keep stirring from time to time to stop the relish from sticking to the bottom of the pan.

4. Remove from the heat and discard the bay leaves before spooning into hot, sterilized jars. This relish must be stored in the refrigerator even if unopened, but will keep for up to 4 months.

ONION & REDCURRANT RELISH

This truly irresistible combination of sweet red onions and sharp redcurrants can be eaten with spicy sausages or soft goat's cheese.

INGREDIENTS *Makes 400g/14oz*

2 tbsp olive oil

2 red onions, diced

1 red pepper, deseeded and diced

1 red chilli, deseeded and chopped

2 garlic cloves, chopped

5cm/2in fresh root ginger, peeled and finely chopped

200ml/7fl oz red wine vinegar

140g/5oz light brown sugar

1 tsp five-spice powder

1 tsp salt

200g/7oz redcurrants, stalks removed

METHOD

1. Heat the olive oil in a large pan and add the diced onions and red pepper. Cook over a medium heat for 5–8 minutes or until the onions have softened and started to turn brown. Remove the onion and peppers from the pan and set aside.

2. Put the chilli, garlic and ginger into the pan along with half the quantity of vinegar. Bring to the boil, then turn down the heat and simmer for 2–3 minutes. Add the onion and pepper mixture, plus the remaining vinegar, sugar, five-spice powder and salt. Bring the mixture back to the boil, then allow to cook at a rolling boil for about 5 minutes or until the mixture has thickened.

3. Turn down the heat, add the redcurrants and simmer for about 5 minutes or until the redcurrants have burst and the liquid is syrupy.

4. Remove from the heat and pour into hot, sterilized jars. Cover and seal while hot. Keep this relish in the refrigerator for up to 3 weeks.

PLUM & CHERRY RELISH

This is an excellent combination of fruity flavours that will enhance any rich poultry dish such as duck or goose.

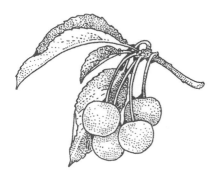

INGREDIENTS *Makes 900g/2lb*

1 tbsp olive oil

2 shallots, finely chopped

350g/12 oz red plums, stoned and chopped

350g/12 oz red cherries, pitted and halved

2 tbsp dry sherry

60ml/2fl oz red wine vinegar

1 tbsp balsamic vinegar

2 bay leaves

1 cinnamon stick

the zest of 1 lemon

100g/3½oz demerara sugar

METHOD

1. Heat the oil in a large stainless steel pan and cook the chopped shallots gently until they are soft, stirring from time to time.

2. Add the prepared plums and cherries to the pan along with all the remaining ingredients and slowly cook the mixture, stirring continuously, until the sugar has completely dissolved.

3. Increase the heat and bring the mixture to a brisk boil. Cook, uncovered, for 15 minutes or until the relish has a thick consistency and the fruit is softened.

4. Remove and discard the bay leaves and cinnamon stick and spoon the relish into hot, sterilized jars. Seal immediately, then add a label and store the relish in the refrigerator once the jars are cold.

SPICY PINEAPPLE RELISH

This relish goes extremely well with gammon. It can also be eaten as a starter with homemade flat breads.

INGREDIENTS *Makes 250g/9oz*
225g/8oz fresh pineapple
1 tbsp olive oil
1 small onion, finely chopped
1 red chilli, sliced, with seeds
½ tsp mustard seeds
½ tsp cumin seeds
½ tsp fennel seeds
2cm/¾in fresh root ginger, peeled
    and grated
115g/4oz raisins
225g/8oz sugar
1 tsp salt
1 tbsp lemon juice
90ml/3fl oz water

METHOD
1. To prepare the pineapple, slice it lengthways into quarters and cut out the tough core. Cut away the skin and chop the flesh into small pieces.
2. Heat the olive oil in a large saucepan and add the onion, red chilli and mustard, cumin and fennel seeds. Cook over a medium heat for 5–6 minutes or until the onion is starting to go soft and the seeds are giving off their aromatic scent.
3. Add the pineapple, ginger, raisins, sugar and salt and cover the pan with a lid. Allow it to simmer on a low heat for a further 5–6 minutes, stirring occasionally to make sure the sugar has dissolved.
4. Add the lemon juice and water and cook, uncovered, for 30–35 minutes until the water has evaporated and the relish is thick.
5. Ladle the relish into hot, sterilized jars and seal immediately. Once it is cool, label and store.

SWEET & SOUR TOMATO RELISH

This relish gives a zing to grilled chicken or chops, and is a must for anyone who loves the combination of sweet and sour.

INGREDIENTS *Makes 250g/9oz*

4 large ripe tomatoes
1 tbsp olive oil
1 onion, finely chopped
1 eating apple, peeled, cored
   and finely chopped
1 garlic clove, finely chopped
2 tbsp tomato purée
1 tbsp balsamic vinegar
1 tbsp brown sugar
1 red chilli, finely sliced
salt and pepper to taste

METHOD

1. Drop the tomatoes into boiling water for 2 minutes, then remove and leave to cool. When cool enough to handle, peel off the skins and chop the flesh into small pieces.

2. Heat the oil in a large pan, add the onion and apple and cook until the onion is soft and just starting to brown. Add the garlic and cook for a further minute.

3. Add the tomatoes to the pan and cook on a high heat for 2 minutes or until the mixture has blended and softened.

4. Add the tomato purée, balsamic vinegar, sugar and chilli and mix thoroughly. Season with salt and pepper and remove from the heat.

5. Transfer the mixture to hot, sterilized jars and seal. Store in the refrigerator and eat within two months of making.

VARIATION

If you prefer a creamier relish, simply put the cooked mixture into a blender and whizz until smooth.

TOMATO & HORSERADISH RELISH

This condiment goes well with both fish and meat, the fresh
horseradish adding a punch to the flavour.

INGREDIENTS *Makes 900g/2lb*

1.8kg/4lb ripe tomatoes, skinned
    and roughly chopped
1 large onion, roughly chopped
2 large eating apples, peeled,
    cored and chopped
450ml/15fl oz red wine vinegar
2 tsp pickling spices
2 tsp salt
½ tsp cayenne pepper
450g/1lb soft brown sugar
3 tbsp grated fresh horseradish

METHOD

1. Put the tomatoes, onion and
apples into a saucepan over
a low heat. Cover and cook
for about 40 minutes, stirring
occasionally, until the vegetables
have been reduced to a pulp.
2. In a separate pan, boil the
vinegar with the pickling spices
for about 10 minutes, covered, to
allow the flavours to infuse.

3. Strain the infused vinegar into
the tomato mixture, then add the
salt and cayenne pepper. Boil
the mixture until it is reduced to
a thick, creamy consistency, then
turn down the heat and add the
sugar and horseradish. Cook for
10 minutes, stirring constantly,
until the sugar has dissolved.
4. Pour into hot, sterilized jars or
bottles and seal. Once it is cool,
label and store.

TOP TIP

When grating horseradish,
make sure your kitchen is
well ventilated, wear rubber
gloves and avoid touching
your eyes.

CRANBERRY KETCHUP

This is a wonderful condiment with meats, especially poultry. Store it for 2 weeks before eating to allow all the flavours to blend.

INGREDIENTS *Makes 1.2 litres/2 pints*
900g/2lb fresh cranberries
1 onion, finely chopped
1 tsp celery seeds
1 tsp mustard seeds
1 tsp whole allspice
1 cinnamon stick
½ tsp black peppercorns
2 bay leaves
250ml/8fl oz white wine vinegar
450g/1lb granulated sugar

METHOD

1. Place the cranberries and onion in a large saucepan and pour in enough water to cover. Bring to the boil then reduce the heat and simmer for 20–30 minutes, stirring occasionally, until the cranberries have become mushy.

2. Put the cranberry and onion mixture into a blender and whizz until you have a fine purée.

3. Put the purée into a clean saucepan and cook, uncovered, at a slow boil until the volume is reduced by half.

4. Put the celery, mustard, allspice, cinnamon, peppercorns and bay leaves inside a piece of muslin and tie securely with a piece of string. Add to the saucepan, cover with a lid and simmer for 30 minutes.

5. Remove the spice bag, add the vinegar and sugar and cook, uncovered, over a medium heat, stirring until the sugar has dissolved. Continue to cook until the ketchup has become very thick, stirring occasionally to stop it from sticking to the bottom of the pan.

6. Ladle the ketchup into hot, sterilized jars to within 3mm/^{1}/$_8$in from the top, wipe the rims and seal immediately.

GOOSEBERRY KETCHUP

This fruity ketchup gives a lovely twist to hamburgers and hotdogs and makes an interesting change from tomato ketchup and mustard.

INGREDIENTS *Makes 1 litre/1³/4 pints*
900g/2lb ripe gooseberries,
   topped, tailed and halved
3 garlic cloves, crushed
1 tbsp salt
1 tsp cayenne pepper
1 tbsp mustard seeds
900ml/1½ pints white wine
   vinegar
350g/12oz demerara sugar
120g/4oz sultanas

METHOD
1. Put the gooseberries in a large pan and squash them down using a potato masher.

2. Add the remaining ingredients to the gooseberries.
3. Bring the mixture to the boil, stirring continuously until the sugar has dissolved completely. Reduce the heat, cover the pan and simmer for about 30 minutes or until the gooseberries are very soft and have started to absorb the vinegar.
4. Strain the mixture through a fine nylon sieve, discarding any skin or seeds that are left behind.
5. Pour the ketchup into hot, sterilized bottles or jars and seal. Label when cold.

PEPPER & CHILLI KETCHUP

The ancho chillies in this recipe have a sweet, spicy flavour and, blended with roasted red peppers, make a wonderful ketchup.

INGREDIENTS *Makes 600ml/1 pint*

4 large red peppers, quartered and seeds removed

2 onions, chopped

2 cooking apples, peeled, cored and roughly chopped

4 ancho chillies, deseeded and chopped

1 bay leaf

sprig of fresh thyme

600ml/1 pint water

360ml/12fl oz red wine vinegar

100g/3½oz granulated sugar

salt and freshly ground black pepper

METHOD

1. Spread the red pepper quarters on a grill pan, skin side up, and cook under a hot grill until the skins start to char. Allow the peppers to cool completely and then discard the skin and chop the flesh roughly.

2. Put the peppers, onions, apples, chillies, bay leaf and thyme into a pan and add the water. Bring to the boil, then cover and simmer for 30–40 minutes or until the vegetables have softened.

3. Remove the bay leaf, transfer the mixture to a blender and whizz until smooth. Rub the mixture through a fine nylon sieve, discarding any pulp that will not go through.

4. Return the purée to a clean pan, add the vinegar, sugar, salt and pepper and bring to a gentle simmer, stirring until the sugar has dissolved. Cook uncovered for about 1 hour over a gentle heat, stirring occasionally until the ketchup has thickened and the liquid has evaporated.

5. Fill hot, sterilized jars or bottles with the ketchup and leave to cool before sealing.

PLUM KETCHUP

This fruity, flavourful ketchup makes a delicious sauce for grilled meat or sausages, or barbecued kebabs.

INGREDIENTS *Makes 1.2 litres/2 pints*
1.8kg/4lb ripe red plums, stoned
   and roughly chopped
2 onions, finely chopped
225g/8oz granulated sugar
150g/5½oz dark brown sugar
1 tsp salt
1½ tsp cinnamon
1½ tsp mustard powder
1 tsp freshly grated nutmeg
½ tsp ground cloves
¼ tsp ground allspice
450ml/15fl oz cider vinegar

METHOD

1. Put the prepared plums into a stainless steel pan with the chopped onions and about 1cm/½in water. Bring to the boil, then reduce the heat and simmer for about 30 minutes or until the plums and onions are soft.

2. Rub the plum mixture through a fine nylon sieve, discarding any skin left in the sieve.

3. Put the purée back into a clean pan and add the remaining ingredients. Heat slowly, stirring continuously until all the sugar has dissolved, and then simmer the mixture uncovered for about 1–1½ hours until the liquid has evaporated and the ketchup has thickened.

4. Pour the ketchup into hot, sterilized bottles or jars and seal immediately.

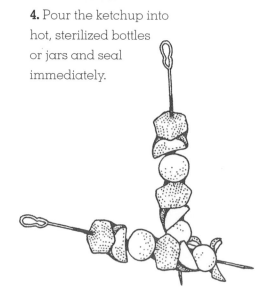

TOMATO KETCHUP

This rich homemade ketchup knocks the socks off any you can buy in the shops and goes very well with oven-baked fish and chips and other traditional favourites.

INGREDIENTS *Makes 500ml/16fl oz*
2 onions, finely chopped
2 kg/4½lb ripe tomatoes, roughly chopped
2 garlic cloves, chopped
150ml/5fl oz red wine vinegar
100ml/3½fl oz water
½ tsp black peppercorns
1 blade of mace
1 tsp ground allspice
2 cloves
2 bay leaves
1 tbsp light brown sugar

METHOD
1. Put the onions, tomatoes, garlic, 60ml/2fl oz of the vinegar and the water into a large saucepan over a medium heat. Cover and cook for about 40 minutes, stirring occasionally, until the vegetables are reduced to a pulp.
2. Pour the remaining vinegar into another saucepan, add the peppercorns, mace, allspice, cloves and bay leaves and cook, covered, over a low heat for 10 minutes. Remove the pan from the heat and set aside.
3. Put the tomato mixture into a blender and whizz until you have a smooth purée. Rub the purée through a fine nylon sieve into a clean saucepan, leaving behind only the skins and seeds.
4. Strain the infused vinegar into the tomato purée, add the sugar and heat slowly, stirring, until the sugar has dissolved. Turn up the heat and cook at a fast simmer until the ketchup has reduced to a thick consistency.
5. Remove the ketchup from the heat and pour into sterilized bottles or jars. Seal immediately and label when cool.

INDEX

....

INDEX